Wayfarer, North Carolina

Seven Short Stories
of
Character and Consequences

J.L. Baumann

Printed in The United States of America
Link Printing, Groveland, Florida 34736

ISBN 978-1-941880-45-6

~ First Edition ~

Introduction

"Oh those small town politics. They're the same everywhere. And it doesn't make any difference which town you come from either. They're all the same," The gray haired woman spoke up from across the table from me.

She had come to this "financial seminar" for a free meal, same as me and everyone else in the room, but really had no intention of investing her retirement money with this company. She had come with her husband, who was the quiet one of the two, after receiving the same glossy oversized postcard invitation in the mail as I. We were given a choice of which place you wanted to claim your free dinner, —the "all you can eat" buffet hall, or the franchise seafood restaurant. Although I did not have a great penchant for fish, I knew that the seating would be far more comfortable at the seafood place, along with the less slothful as compatriots, and so I ventured into the maritime world of somewhat above average cuisine.

Seated all together at one long table there were perhaps sixteen of us who were there, being fattened up for the anticipated kill, —but what the heck, who didn't know that. We were allowed to be fed first and as the soporific effect of the food took over everyone now began to finally relax. This was where the folks would start to share the commonality of their age, not in the physical sense, but in the anecdotal collective. This was why I really came.

"I don't think that anyone would argue with that," I responded to her political observation, "but still, you have to take into account the individual, the reason why people do what they do. I am more of the mind that the politics are the same everywhere, small town or big city. Now, the one primary exception, as I see it, is the personal touch. In the case of the small town, it is more likely that one actually knows the players and are more likely to be personally acquainted with them. They

know where they work, where their whole family came from, and even what grades they got in high school, — a friend or antagonist, you still wonder about them today.

"I'll bet you that everyone here has at least one good story about somebody you went to high school with," I subsequently proposed to everyone who was listening, "a story about someone that you really knew, or perhaps still know today, that is literally worth writing down. Even if you were raised in a big city, it's still about your neighborhood most of all, a sort of small town within a town, so to speak," I provocatively suggested, adding a little more bait to my hook.

"Are you some kind of writer?" the woman now asked of me straight away.

"Actually, more of an editor than anything," I replied. "Although I do have some published pieces," I added.

"Is that so?" she questioned.

"Yeah, for thirty years, I was a magazine editor, but now I am retired, just like you," I told her.

"Do you still write? I mean like, for yourself?" she pressed on.

"Well, sure. Right now I'm working on a book of short stories," I responded.

"You know, you ought to listen to some of the stories my husband has," she offered. "He used to own a small town restaurant way back in the seventies. You should hear them. Maybe they are something you can use."

"Sure, —I guess I could do that," I hesitantly agreed, not letting on that her proposal was the offer I'd been looking for.

"So, say something, honey," she said, nudging the gray haired man next to her."

"We live in the Golfside Estates, down off highway eighty-six. Do you know where it is?" the plain spoken man sitting next to her asked.

"Yeah, I know where it is," I told him.

"I'm free on Tuesdays, usually. We could meet in the clubhouse, if you want," the man proposed.

"I know where it is. About two in the afternoon?" I suggested.

"That's good for me, —and by the way, my name is Maurice," he pleasantly offered.

It was after listening to Maurice tell his stories that I had become a firm believer that if anyone who wanted to know anything at all about humanity, all they needed to do is work for a while in a restaurant. "The restaurant is society's greatest forum," Maurice theorized, "and I mean the world over. You see, it involves the greatest addiction of all—eating. Drugs are not, and neither is smoking or alcohol. Those things you can live without. But eating is the one habit you can't," he categorially stated. "Then, when you add to that how much people are always looking for someplace to be socially, there you have it, -the real purpose of a restaurant," he proposed with a 'cat that ate the canary' grin.

These stories are a testament to all those who are still in recovery from ever having been employed in, or even mildly associated with, such a public concern.

Table of Contents

The White Glove Inspection

It was three in the afternoon when he came in. It was always three in the afternoon when he came in, for that was when the restaurant was virtually empty, and he knew that. After all, it was his business to know this because he was the state's longest surviving field inspector for both its ubiquitous and all pervasive health department. And only standing at five foot two, he was also the shortest. Mr. Ceagan was his name and claimed to be the proudest of all French epicureans. This, he also claimed, gave him not just the legal right to perform his function, but gave him a God given mandate to do so as well. According to his philosophy, which was stated with no small degree of levity, all Frenchmen were born with two distinct proclivities: one was to be the supreme judges of world's greatest culinary dishes, and the other was to recognize the natural beauty of women.

It was hard to tell his age because of his perfectly manicured jet black hair and his matching pencil thin mustache, but from the weathering of his face he appeared to be at least in his sixties. His shoes were patent leather, his shirts were always white-on-white and crisply starched. The tie he wore was also always the same. It thin, black, and clearly displayed his initials CC, monogrammed upon it in gold. He had a broad, congenial smile and for an official of the state he always seemed much too gregarious for the gravity of his position.

It was obvious that his vocation was his life's work, and although he was most affable, he took his responsibilities seriously. He had a great deal of knowledge and often spoke of his days in training aboard the grand cruise ships of the thirties when they were considered to be the pinnacle of luxury for the wealthy. He was above the mind set of being officious as he likened himself to be a professor of sorts, a master in the field of Epicurean arts. This, of course, involved the distasteful task of

handing out a poor grade occasionally, but one had to only listen to his advice and correct what needed to be corrected, and all was forgiven.

"This can't be Charlie's Restaurant," was heard from the kitchen, one bright and excruciating hot summer day, after the only waitress left on duty had gone to the storeroom, looking for a pack of paper napkins for the table dispensers.

"Oh, hello," the proprietor said as he came out into the dining room. "How are you doing, Mr. Ceagan?"

"Oh, I don't know. I thought that this place served the coldest beer in town, but I don't see anyone out here to serve me one," the Mr. Ceagan spiritedly taunted, pretending to be mystified in looking around as if —"poof" one would appear.

"Well, sir, if you just take a seat in the booth over there in the corner, I'll get Betty to round one up for you. And then I'll join you, okay?" the young entrepreneur proposed to the jovial inspector.

"Now that sounds good, because I sure don't want to have to go back outside in that heat again," Mr. Ceagan replied, turning to take a seat in the booth as offered.

"I'll go get Betty now," said restaurateur respectfully, promptly leaving for the kitchen.

The owner's name of the establishment was, in fact, not Charlie. It was actually Maurice. But when he had purchased the place about a year earlier, in an effort to retain its current customer base, he decided that it would not be wise for him to to change the establishment's name. As far as his own name was concerned, he simply told everyone to just call him Bo. He was only a young man of twenty-five, and most of the patrons did not believe he was even that, given his even younger appearance.

Bo had actually worked his way through college in the restaurant business, from dishwasher to cook, and then to manager, and yet as he was quick to find out, owning his own place was a totally different story. This was his first venture in trying to become a businessman, and

though working harder than ever, he knew he did not know everything. This is why he was always grateful to see Mr. Ceagan, for every time he was inspected he always learned something new, a new tip, a new way to save money, or especially what was becoming the new trend.

Betty was a dark haired, pretty young girl, who, although was plain spoken and simple in manner, had the most striking green eyes. She neither hustled in her service to the customers, nor was she slow. For all intents and purposes however, she appeared focused upon her duties, deliberate in her efforts, and the customers felt comfortable in her charge. She had moved to the small town with her boyfriend after graduating high school from a large manufacturing city, and because he could not find any work that suited him, he returned without her. She liked her job, and even more important, she liked having her own money to spend. Working at Charlie's was the first job she ever had, and the independence it fostered produced within her an undeniable state of euphoria. She was happy in her job, and did precisely what she was told.

"Mr. Ceagan just came in. He's sitting over in the corner booth. You can finish wrapping the silver later. I want you to go and get him a draft, and then talk to him a while. —He likes girls. So go and make him feel good. Keep him occupied and talk to him 'till I get out there. I'm going to clean up the kitchen a little before he inspects this place and then I'll be right out," Bo instructed, leaving the supply room to put away the stuffed peppers he was preparing.

"Here you are, Mr. Ceagan," Betty announced minutes later, putting down a cardboard coaster and a cold glass of beer on the table before him.

"Oh, thank you, dear," Mr. Ceagan acknowledged.

"Are you going to inspect us, today?" Betty asked.

"I am always inspecting, young lady, —and here's to you," Mr. Ceagan toasted pleasantly, then taking a drink.

"So, where have you been? We didn't see you last month," Betty questioned with a concerned tone in her voice.

"Oh, I am only scheduled to come here every two months. You see, the county is supposed to inspect you one month and the state is to inspect you the next. Then we are supposed to send each other the reports," the inspector factually explained, finally relaxing back in the booth to get more comfortable.

"Do you want anything to eat?" Betty inquired amiably.

"Oh no, dear. I'm fine," Mr. Ceagan told her with a small wave of his hand. "So, how is life treating you? I imagine that a young pretty girl like you has your pick of the all fellows, don't you?" he affably proposed.

"No, I just work here," Betty answered benignly. "I moved here with my boyfriend, but he left to go back home. I stayed here because I like it here. Right now, I am saving up so I can get a new car."

"Really?" Mr. Ceagan impulsively responded. "What kind of car are you looking to buy?" he questioned, obviously in great interest.

"A GTO," Betty answered succinctly.

"Really?" Mr. Ceagan responded in surprise. "I have an Alpine Tiger," he then told her proudly.

"What's that?" Betty asked.

"It's a small European sports car that is used in racing. It's only a two seater, but it's extremely fast. Of course I don't race it. I only use it for touring around. I keep it in the garage and only take it out on the weekends. Other than that, I drive my old Chevy Impala out there," Mr. Ceagan stated matter-of-factly, taking another sip from his glass.

"So, Mr. Ceagan, how are you doing, now?" Bo interrupted, coming up from behind Betty and sitting down in the booth across from the courteously attended inspector. "I'll have a cup of coffee," he told Betty in dismissing her.

"Better than I was before," Mr. Ceagan answered with a wry little smile, "How's business?" he questioned in turn.

"Always getting better, Mr. Ceagan," Bo responded. "I'm ready whenever you are," he said to the fastidious little man.

"All in good time, my son," Mr. Ceagan answered, taking up his glass again.

"Well, anytime you are ready," Bo responded pleasantly.

"Here's your coffee, sir," Betty broke in, putting down the heavy ceramic mug on the table. "Anything else?"

"No, but thank you, anyway," Bo responded politely.

"Okay, I'll be in the kitchen, then," Betty announced before leaving.

It was then that Mr. Ceagan reached down onto the seat beside him and retrieved the clipboard he never failed to be without. Next, placing it square on the table before him, he took out a pen from his top shirt pocket, and clicked it at the ready. Meanwhile, the young man across the table, at the same time, had reached out for the stainless creamer and the glass sugar container at the far end of the table, and used them both. Finally, after the two of them had gotten fully situated, Mr. Ceagan began.

"You know that no one ever gets a perfect score, don't you?" the inspector asked in a tone of complete sobriety.

"Yes, sir. I can imagine that, Mr. Ceagan," Bo answered respectfully.

"And it is because of that, in order to save us time of having me to unnecessarily go through the motions, that I have already almost completed your inspection right here," Mr. Ceagan unexpectedly informed Bo, pointing to the form on the clipboard with his pen.

"You mean you are not going to actually inspect me today?" Bo asked in mild surprise.

"Oh, au contraire, like I said, we are going to complete your inspection right now, —only this time we are going to do it from right from here, that's all," he corrected with a slightly patronizing smile.

"Well how are we going to do that?" Bo asked, completely taken aback.

"Like I said, you know that no one gets one hundred percent, so I have written you up for two things here that I want you to correct," he stated officiously. "The first one, is I want you to buy two small garbage cans to put those fifty pound bags of potatoes and onions in when they come in from the purveyors, for no matter how hard you try, sooner or later, they will bring in the bugs with them. This way, it will at least keep them contained so they don't go all over the place. I am not going to write you up for the bugs, only that you need to take some better preventive measures, that's all," he said informatively.

"I understand," Bo affirmed.

"Then the second one is that number ten can opener you have back there. If you pull it up and turn it over you will see all kinds of material stuck within its gears. You need to take it and run it under the hot water and clean it thoroughly on a more regular basis," Mr. Ceagan instructed. "When was the last time you did?" he then asked, point blank.

"To tell you the truth, Mr. Ceagan, I never have. It just gets wiped down. I mean it isn't used when you actually make anything, so I never thought about it," Bo honestly replied.

"No one ever does, son," Mr. Ceagan smiled in the vindication of his expertise, taking his pen and making a few notations on the form of his clipboard. "Now, I already have written down these two violations, but I still need to ask you a few more questions, okay?" Mr. Ceagan said in an automatic fashion, not looking up from his paperwork.

"Okay," Bo responded.

"You aren't selling anything on the menu that isn't what it says it is, like horse meat or shark are you?" the inspector asked.

"No, Mr. Ceagan, who would do that?" Bo responded in amazement.

"Oh, you'd be surprised," Mr. Ceagan commented, raising his eyebrows in all seriousness. "There is one of the larger seafood chains

around here that has the habit of buying grouper by the ton and then selling it on their menus as both bass and snapper as well, depending how they filet it. They claimed that snapper could be any fish that "snapped" on a fish line," he mentioned with an exasperated sigh, looking off and away for a moment and lightly shaking his head. "Anyway, one more thing is, —you have a sign in the bathroom telling all your employees to wash your hands don't you?" he questioned assumptively.

"Yes, I do, sir," Bo answered straightaway.

"Good," said Mr. Ceagan approvingly, signing the form in front of him. "Okay, your report is all finished now, and you got a ninety-three. That's not so bad," he commented with a shrug. "Here, you need to sign right there," he directed, turning around the clipboard and pointing to the bottom of the form with his pen, then handing it out for the young man to take.

"Is that it, then?" Bo asked politely, after returning the signed report.

"Oh, no, my son. That was just part one of your inspection today," Mr. Ceagan revealed, putting the clipboard back onto the seat next to him again, relaxing back and taking another sip from his libation.

"What's the other part?" questioned Bo, having no idea whatsoever what Mr. Ceagan was going to do next.

"Okay, here," Mr. Ceagan responded, shifting in his seat and reaching into his back left pocket. "I want you to take a good look at these now," he said, tossing down a set of white leather gloves in front of his patiently attentive pupil.

"Boy, these are pretty nice," Bo remarked in looking them over.

"Here, hand them back to me," Mr. Ceagan directed casually, holding out his right hand. "You see, these aren't just an ordinary pair of gloves," he underscored as he took them back. "These are a set of world class gloves. The best racing gloves in the world," he stressed, dramatically wagging them about. "The purpose of them is to keep your hands from slipping on the wheel of your sports car when you are driving in the

Grand Prix. Now I brought them here specifically to show you exactly what a white glove inspection really is," he stated candidly. "Are you ready?" he then questioned engagingly.

"Sure, go on Mr. Ceagan," Bo replied receptively.

"First of all, I want you to understand that they are made of the finest Italian kidskin, hand-crafted to the exact measurements of my hands, and my hands only, —soft and supple as no other leather in the world," Mr. Ceagan began solemnly. "Now, if you look on the outside of the seams, you will notice that they are stitched from the inside," he demonstratively pointed out. "That keeps the fingers from annoyingly catching against each other when you are trying to steer your roadster along the winding mountain roads. Now, take a look at the inside. See the silk lining?" he further questioned.

"Yes sir, they sure are nice," the young man commented.

"Well, that is so they will slide on your hands smoothly and not get chaffed from the inside stitching when you are again, driving your roadster around the mountain roads, —like I mentioned before," Mr. Ceagan animatedly reinforced.

"I see," Bo replied as his instructor slipped on the gloves.

"And now, you see this little pearl snap at the wrist where the cuff of the glove is?" Mr. Ceagan questioned.

"Yes, I see that, too," Bo solicitously replied.

"So now, when I snap them closed, you also notice how naturally snug they become?" Mr. Ceagan asked while clenching his fists tightly, causing the leather to audibly stretch to the form of his hands.

"They sure are beautiful," Bo complemented.

"Now here is your lesson, young man," Mr. Ceagan prefaced. "You now have been instructed on how to inspect the finest pair of racing gloves in the world. You know of the finest of materials, you know of the finest hand-craftsmanship provided to make them, and you know of the specific purpose for which they were made. That, sir, is a white glove

inspection!" he vociferously declared. "And if you even begin to think, like in the movies, that I would smear them the across the greasy tops of those refrigerators you have back there, which no one ever cleans any more than the gears in that can opener of yours, you have got to be out of your mind!" he exclaimed in animated shock.

The Last Deal

Mr. Kent was the owner of small used car lot who, on occasion, would come into the small town's local restaurant for lunch. He was a balding man in his late forties, and if there was ever a "hail-fellow-well-met" person, he was the one. Casually dressed, he was the quintessential picture of a middle-aged businessman. He, like so many other residents of the town, ended up settling there because his last tour of duty was at the large military base nearby and had gotten comfortable with the town's easy going lifestyle.

Pleasant, more than affable, Mr. Kent was also the typification of the mild mannered mid-westerner. With no discernable accent such as folks have from the northeast part of the country, or some of the rural areas of the south, he blended right into the community like the brown pair of loafers he wore. Soft-spoken, smoothly polished and practiced, at first he gave the illusion that he was a genuine heartfelt person in every respect, but those who were personally acquainted with him knew him to be the most calculating man they had ever known.

Whether it was out of boredom or simply the feeling of the elation from having another conquest under his belt, every so often he would place an ad in the newspaper for a secretary which he never had intention of hiring. The ad always included the phrase "no experience necessary" in looking for the young and the desperate to apply. The "interview" was always scheduled at eleven o'clock, at which time the applicant was given a two page application and a six page "aptitude test" which was as nonsensical as it was inane. Patiently, Mr. Kent would sit at his desk, pretending to be busy while waiting for the girl to complete the test. Once the documents were completed and handed back to him, he would briefly peruse them with a doctorial "hmm…" and then summarily place them down on his desk, casually glancing at his watch.

"Oh my God," Mr. Kent would begin. "It's lunchtime! I don't have time to go over your application now. Do you want to go to lunch with me and then we can go over it after we come back?"

Moreover, as the answer was usually "yes," he would then take the young girl to the nearest chain restaurant where he had acquired a "Buy a Lunch, Get a Lunch Free" coupon. The conversation was always the same. First he would ask about her general welfare in a concerned fashion and then he would questioned her motivations for applying for the job. This was followed by a testament of his own success and his plans to expand his business. Then, as if he had just gotten a brainstorm, he would ask the girl if she would mind appearing in his new TV commercial that he was about to launch, therein hoping to reveal to what degree her vanity could be exploited. Sometimes the ploy would work and consequently gain him the sexual favors that he was after, and sometimes it did not. Regardless, the ridiculous aptitude test that was filled out was never graded, for it was only a sales ploy in the first place.

It did not take long for Mr. Kent's reputation to infiltrate the small town's world of salesmen and accordingly had attracted a following of like-minded characters who admired his craftiness in the world of "deal making." Thus, when the other salesmen in the area wished to expand their repertoire of closing techniques, they would seek him out, so perchance they would be able to glean a new idea from the master. The price for this opportunity was of course, his lunch.

Occasionally, Mr. Kent would have fishing parties on his thirty-six foot cabin cruiser which he kept docked at the coastal marina. Whether the boat was bought for self-aggrandizement purposes or because he actually liked to go fishing was irrelevant, for the truth was that no one personally cared. All of the invitees on such occasions were invariably called "my good friends," and as such Mr. Kent limited the required contributions to be no more than the expense that it took to actually take the boat out, such as the gas, the bait, and the food, of which the

aggregate cost would be divvied amongst his guests "fairly." He also graciously informed everyone that since it was he who was absorbing all of the overhead, he need not be included in the sharing these costs.

It was actually Pete, Mr. Kent's right hand salesman, who had first come into the small restaurant that was only a block and a half away from the car lot. Pete was a short and overweight husky man who was retired from the army at thirty-eight. He was from Johnstown, Pennsylvania, and on many occasion recanted the loss of much of his family in the great flood of 1889. This fact of life's hopelessness, he proffered to anyone who would listen, was the primary reason he joined the Army at eighteen in the first place, not because of his passion to fight the Germans for the love of his country, candidly adding to his reasoning that he would rather be shot to death than die drowning.

In the beginning of his tour he served in the infantry, but after the war he was successfully accepted to be retrained as a radar tech. Eventually, he became a Specialist Sergeant whose job it was to install all types of radar equipment from the deserts of Iran to the frozen regions of Greenland. He had never gotten married and lived alone in a single-bedroom mobile home. It wasn't that he did not have an affinity for the women, it was more that he was an odd duck that led to singularity, consequently causing the opposite sex to warily avoid him. Also, for his part, he was simply more concerned with his get rich quick schemes than anything else. He was constantly trying to invent all sorts of cockamamie ventures to get people involved in, and although most everyone regarded him as being harmless in an overall weird sort of way, no one would publically admit to being truly associated with him in any manner.

With a large square head and a set of even larger horned-rimmed glasses, he looked exactly like someone who should be installing radar equipment, not selling cars for Mr. Kent. Nonetheless, that was his current employment, and since the restaurant was a convenient place to break the monotony of his otherwise droll and uneventful existence,

he came in almost every day for lunch by himself. He also was one of the few people who also came in for dinner, for the daytime patrons were usually a completely different crowd, both in habit and desires. He therefore had become a "regular" in all respects.

"I am going to have a draught tonight, and I think I will even order a steak," Pete said one evening after he had taken up residence on the twelve seat counter at the back of the room, directly next to the kitchen entrance.

It was barely past five o'clock in the afternoon, and except for a solitary couple in the far booth, Pete was the only patron in the restaurant.

"Boy, that's a new one," Bo had commented from behind the counter. "Did somebody invest in your "Chick N' Fat" venture?" he asked facetiously.

"Oh, heck no, I sold a car today and made an extra three hundred bucks," he responded with as much swagger as a corpulent man could display.

"Well, let me get your draught, and then tell me about it," Bo said, turning to the tap behind him. "Isn't that a little more than Mr. Kent pays you?" he asked over his shoulder while drawing the beer, "I thought he only gave you a 'yard,' as you guys call it," he further commented.

"Yeah, well, I'll tell you about it if you just keep it between ourselves, okay?" Pete offered in a more secretive tone when his beer was delivered before him.

"Sure, Pete, what do I care?" Bo replied.

"Okay then, if you don't tell anyone, I'll tell you," Pete reiterated.

"Who am I going to tell? Go on, just tell me," Bo plainly directed.

"Well, this customer came in the other day and was looking for an old Chevy Corvair, of all things," Pete began. "I guess he collects them. Anyway, of course Mr. Kent didn't have one, but I knew of one of the dealers who did. So, I went to the dealer and paid him cash for it as if it was for Mr. Kent, —that way, I got it wholesale. Then I called up

the guy and he came over to my trailer and paid me for it. I made three hundred bucks off the deal," he boasted with and sly grin, saluting Bo with his beer mug in celebration.

"Isn't that kind of cheating your employer?" Bo suggested.

"Not at all," was the immediate and unconscionable reply. "You see, he always tries to cheat me, and I, in turn, just try to cheat him back. That's how it works. Don't you know that?" Pete stated in self-justification, intonating that Bo was naive.

"No, I don't," Bo sternly replied.

"Well, follow me here for a second," Pete subsequently proposed. "If I would have told him about the deal, he would have made it himself and only given me a hundred bucks. He would have said that it was his money and his connections, and that these factors are more important than my efforts. He wouldn't have even split the deal with me. And after all, it was me this time who knew where the Corvair was in the first place. He didn't even have a clue where to find one, and never would have either, because this particular dealer that had it, can't stand the sight of him," he tagged on, amused at the irony.

"You see, you don't understand," Pete continued in a patronizing manner. "It's always the same with him; after a sale is made, I'm supposed to get a percentage over what it was bought and cleaned up for, but he always adds on what he calls 'pack' to the expenses and takes it out of my share. Then, he lies to me and says his accountant told him he has to do it. Then, to even make it worse, as far as I know, he doesn't even have an accountant," he stressed. "He finagles the books all by himself. So, there you have it, —he tries to cheat me, so I cheat him in return. And that's the way it is," he maintained, nonchalantly leaning back and taking another drink of his beer.

"And by the way, that's the way it is all over the world," Pete epilogued after lowering his glass. "Believe me, I've been all over the

world and I know," he reemphasized. "You'll see when you get older," he condescendingly predicted.

"Oh, I don't know about that," Bo responded, lightly in disagreement, "And let me tell you, too, while we're on the subject," he began to elaborate. " I am not exactly a fan of Mr. Kent, either," he confessed. "He came in a couple of months back with some other guys and asked me to give them all a free beer, just for him bringing them here. Of course I told him that I wasn't going to do it," he stated as a matter-of-fact. "Then, once they were all finished, Mr. Kent said out loud, so that even the people sitting next to them could hear it, 'I don't know exactly what it is, but the food in here just isn't the same as it was the last time I came in,' and that I 'must be doing something different,' adding that he didn't think that he would be coming back anymore. To me it didn't make any difference. I put the check down and it was paid regardless," he shrugged in unconcern. "So I couldn't care less if he comes back. Actually, I hope he doesn't," he definitively stated.

"So, you do understand," noted Pete.

"Oh yeah, I understand what you are saying, all right. I just don't agree with you, that's all. I don't think that you have to become just like him to make a living. I could never work for someone who is always trying to cheat me out of my wages, even if I could always cheat him back to make up for it. And it's not just a game either. It's still stealing, no matter what you call it, no matter what your justification is," Bo argued. "It's simply no way to live. I believe that whether it's financial or spiritual, everything has it consequences. And I personally think that everyone, sooner or later, will reap what they sow," he qualified respectfully. "Anyway, that's just me," he attached dismissively, ending his point of view. "Well, you want the T-bone, Pete? It's the biggest steak we got," Bo advocated, deliberately changing the subject.

"Yeah, that sounds good," Pete replied, completely unmoved by Bo's opinion.

For the next six months, the subject of Mr. Kent had never come up again, and as predicted by Mr. Kent himself, he did not return, either. Pete's main subject of interest, nevertheless, still went on unabatedly. It was his "Chick N' Fat" project. Quite adamantly, he claimed that there were millions to be made by feeding the chickens the unwanted and discarded walnut shells from the nut industry. Once crushed, he claimed, that when fed to the chickens, it would cause them to grow much faster and fatter than ever. Also, he claimed that he could obtain the nut shells for free.

Pete even went to the expense of buying the chickens and giving them away to a number of the folks who were willing to go along with his venture, and also had the property to raise them. Ergo, this meant that he had to now provide the participants the crushed shells. This was solved, "just to prove a point," by Pete going to the store, buying, shelling, and crushing the walnut shells himself. In the end, his total return was in the neighborhood of four dozen eggs, fresh of course.

Having become one of the dinner's more constant fixtures, Pete had the habit of talking to everyone who happened to have the benefit of, as he saw it, sitting next to him at the counter. Then, if it wasn't him talking about his chicken business, he talked about other such ventures as worm farming for profit and the selling of mink oil cosmetics on the party plan. The one thing that he never did talk about, however, was his employment at the car lot. For whatever reason, he simply never did, —nor did he ever mention Mr. Kent at all. Then, quite unexpectedly, on one torridly humid Thursday morning, no sooner had the front door been unlocked, than in came Pete blurting out the instant he had come through the door, "You won't believe it, Bo, Mr. Kent is dead!"

"Really Pete? Are you kidding me? You can do better than that," Bo replied, believing he was being trifled with.

"No, sir. He's dead all right. Let me sit down at the counter and I'll tell you about it," Pete advanced in the most serious manner.

"Do you want a cup of coffee, Pete?" one of the waitresses asked from behind the eat-on counter where she was laying out the place mats and silverware.

"Yeah, that would be good, I could use one," Pete replied, cumbrously taking a seat across from where the waitress was working. "Thank you," he said after the black and white uniformed waitress put down his coffee and promptly left to resume her chores.

"So, Mr. Kent is dead?" Bo asked, once behind the counter himself. "How'd it happen? Was he in an accident or something?" he questioned, more out of interest than anything.

"No, he died of a heart attack last Friday night I guess," Pete answered soberly.

"Well, how old was he? He didn't seem that old," Bo remarked.

"No, he wasn't. He was only forty-eight," Pete confirmed after taking a drink from his coffee.

"And you just found out? I mean, you said he passed away last Friday night, and today it's already Thursday. How could that happen?" Bo asked in puzzlement.

"That's the thing," Pete replied, explicitly pointing his finger up in the air, "No one even knew he was dead until yesterday,"

"But how could that happen?" Bo skeptically requestioned, "What about when he didn't show up for work?"

"I open the place in the morning," Pete replied factually. "And if it is a slow week, sometimes he doesn't come in at all until Friday when he has to give me something for being there."

"But what about his wife? And what about everyone else who knew him? Didn't they miss him? And where was he when he had his heart attack anyway?" Bo continued over the strangeness of the circumstances.

"He was found out on his boat, dead as a mackerel," Pete graphically disclosed. "And you see, no one missed him, because no one really liked him. It's just that simple," Pete straightforwardly added. "Sometimes he

would go and stay on his boat for over a week at a time, completely all by himself, only coming back when he felt like it," he disclosed.

"You're kidding me! You mean his wife didn't go with him, either?" Bo pressed again.

"Nope, not even her," Pete answered succinctly. "From what I understand, she didn't like him anymore than anyone else did. And that I got from the guy who had worked at the lot before me. He told me that the money he opened the car lot with came from his wife after her father had died. Then, after he paid cash for his boat, and there was no money left from her inheritance, he treated her like crap," he related dispassionately. "And you want to know something else? As far as I know, I don't even think his wife ever saw boat. I've been on it a couple times, and I sure never saw her," he flatly declared. "In fact, if you really want to know, I've never seen her at all, ever, —until yesterday when she came onto the lot and told me he was dead," he testified, as if giving a deposition.

"So, who found him, then?" Bo questioned further.

"Apparently, he died right after he got on the boat last Friday night. But it wasn't until Tuesday, after the smell had gotten so bad, that someone was forced to investigate. It was then he was found by the marina's manager, stiff as a board, and covered with flies, lying on the inside deck," he related in an apathetic tone, thoughtfully pausing a second while taking another drink of his coffee. "Well, I guess the wifey got to go on the boat after all," he ironically annotated. "Anyway, just the same," he added with a shrug and a slight sardonic grin, "I still gotta hand it to him," he added a complimentary tone, lightly shaking his head. "Before he kicked the bucket, Mr. Kent even arranged to get the best of the funeral people, too," he annotated.

"What do you mean by that?" Bo asked, completely mystified by the incongruence of Pete's sentiments.

"Well, even though he really was a bastard, he was still the best at getting the better end of the deal," Pete said pointedly. "You know those guys that sell those funeral plots?" he rhetorically asked. "They always thought they were the best salesmen, —until they had a tangle with Mr. Kent. Here, I'll explain it for you," he began.

"You see, they advertised one time that they would give away a free grave site to the spouse of any veteran buried there, figuring to sell the veteran his plot for twice the price. So, Mr. Kent went down there with his DD214 and bought the twin grave sites. Finally, after he had it all in writing, and got the deeds recorded, he produced his wife's DD214, because she was also a veteran, and demanded a refund. You see, his wife was an army nurse, honorably discharged, that was how he met her, and therefore he was entitled to a free grave site, too, —because he in turn, was her spouse. And that was his argument.

"Well of course they wouldn't pay off, so Mr. Kent hired a lawyer. Finally, in the end, the funeral people actually capitulated, and not because of his lawyer, but because Mr. Kent threatened to expose the whole scam in the newspaper. And no way in hell did they want that.

"So there you have it. Now he is going to be buried in a grave that he never had to pay for, and all because he was the best at closing the deal. That's all I'm saying," he rationalized with a thin victorious smile, revealing that he believed that Mr. Kent's dealings, no matter how indecent, were nonetheless an accomplishment to be envied.

In the end, after Mr. Kent had finally been interned, and notwithstanding any conversations over the grandeur of his military ceremony, at which his wife, Pete, and the Veterans Honor Guard were the only attendees, his name was never to be brought up at the restaurant again. Bo, however, when buying a new car about six months later, had found out that Mr. Kent's wife had not only remarried within six months of the funeral, but had also sold the boat for practically nothing to a

young married couple in love, just to be rid of it. She had also donated her unwanted gravesite to another veteran who had gratefully thanked her for the gift.

The Judgement

Although Norman for the most part was a lone diner, he never sat at the eat on counter. He was a corner booth person who usually preferred to sit where he had a good view of the whole dining room. He was a gangly sort of man whose interest lay in the study of the Civil War, or as he termed it, "The War of Northern Aggression." This, however, was his hobby study, not his vocation. He was a life insurance and investment professional specializing in retirement accounts.

Norman was an affable man in his early thirties and was a faithful member of the largest Presbyterian Church in the county. He made his living as financial planner, but unlike most others in the profession, he projected the image of being more diligent than aggressive, mainly because he never had to be. His extended family owned a considerable amount of land in the county where some had cattle operations, some were in farming, while still others went into the housing development business. It was seen to that he had a good education, a good car, and an equally good wife who was destined to have two children, one of each brand.

Always adduced in a pin-striped suit and tie, Norman stuck out like a sore thumb in the small country eatery, but everyone was well acquainted his family and he was well treated with respect. Norman not only believed that his Tuesday evening appointments were his luckiest time to write "a piece of business," but considered himself additionally fortunate that the diner's special on that particular day was meatloaf, a meal that he liked far better when it was made by Bo than anyone else, including his wife. Conveniently, nonetheless, Tuesday evening was also when Hawaii Five-O was aired, and being his wife's favorite television program, which Norman couldn't care about less, she was "given the night off" to do with whatever she pleased. This arrangement was a perfect fit.

Bo liked the even-spoken man and considered him one of the best educated folks who came in, which gave him a break in the otherwise social bantering that usually went on between the regular counter independents. Perhaps the greatest commonality the two young men had was that they both graduated college with a minor in history.

The fact that one sold food and the other sold financial services for a living had virtually nothing to with the fundamental focus of their conversations over the very nature of history itself. Was history simply a product of cause and effect? Was the old adage that "He who doesn't learn from history is condemned to repeat" it a truism? Or, is history's entire concept fundamentally based upon economics, as Charles A. Beard proposed? All these topics, and more, were discussed with great self-satisfaction, for both of them knew that their hindsight conclusions could not be challenged by the subjects they chose to pass judgement on.

They thoroughly enjoyed each other's company so much so that Bo would uncharacteristically sit down at Noman's table and drink a coffee after Norman's meal had been delivered, so as to better discuss their shared observations about the idiosyncrasies of the human condition in relation to the past, while subsequently comparing them to their current situations as well.

While Bo provided his stories from a restaurant owner's point of view, Norman told his tales from his financial management experiences. Always, however, their anecdotes had one or two things in common: one, they were true experiences that they had personally witnessed, and two, the stories that they told always had an ending that produced a befittingly derived conclusion.

Normally, Norman was in a causally affable mood when he came in, but on this particular evening when Bo sat down for their customary storytelling, he noticed that his favorite raconteur was in a somber mood.

"What's the problem, Norm?" Bo said when he sat down and noticed the change in his friend's usually composed disposition.

"Oh, I had an appointment to write a policy on someone who reminded me of a sad situation that happened, once. That's all," Norman said sedately.

"So, what's the problem? Didn't you write it?" Bo asked.

"Yeah. I wrote it all alright," Norman confirmed. I've written the guy's whole family, —his brother, his other brother, his mother, — everybody. I was just thinking about his father again, that's all. I really liked the old guy," he pensively looked down with a soft sigh.

"Well, tell me about it," Bo prompted.

"Okay, might as well," Norman acceded, adjusting his position to get more comfortable. "Now, the first time I met his father was when I had a probate case and I had to go before him," he began. "At the time, he was a circuit court judge. I don't know if you ever heard of him, — Judge Lubitt?" he questioned.

"No, Norm. I don't know one judge from another. I never been before one," Bo replied, shrugging his shoulders.

"Oh well, it doesn't make any difference," Norman dismissed. "Regardless, I had this attorney," he continued, "who was also a client of mine, and one day asked for my help in filling out one the court's probate forms because one of his clients had a stock portfolio and it was fairly complicated. Even this judge couldn't figure it out. So there I was. I balanced the account for them, and that was that. I was done," he paused, taking a drink from his coffee.

"Pretty much, that was about it," Norman declared, —until one day, about two years later, the same attorney friend called me up and said that the same judge wanted to see me, personally. This time, however, since the judge had retired from the bench, I was asked if I could to go directly to his law office in the downtown Luella Building, so I said sure.

"His problem was that he had just found out that the life insurance policy he had bought twenty years earlier had no cash value left and was about to lapse. He was livid. He figured that because the company which he bought it from, being one of the largest, became that way because of their honesty. Boy, as he found out, what a joke that is," he noted sarcastically.

"Apparently, a few years back, they rolled all the cash value of his whole life policy over into one of those variable policies where the premiums are paid out of a fund from a cash value investment account, instead of being a direct premium payment. Of course, that's all well and fine when the market is going up, but when it goes down it can be death warmed over, —and that is exactly what happened to him. In any case, he simply trusted the salesman who came over, signed all the papers, and paid no attention to it until he got his lapse notice a couple of weeks ago telling him that the cash value he had accumulated was all but gone, and just to keep it in force his premium would need to be doubled. It was then he had my buddy call me."

"That's horrible," Bo commented.

"Yup, sure is," Norman agreed. "But here's where the real story is," he went on. "You see, the whole situation is a very complicated one. And even though I told the judge that I had no intention of charging him for my time, which he offered to pay, and also knowing that the insurance company would fight him tooth and nail, I decided to help him anyway. So whether it was because I didn't charge him, or he simply took a liking to me, I don't know, but after a while he began to talk to me about all sorts of things, mostly about his own situation. Which of his sons should he give control of his practice to? —for both of them were lawyers. And, why did he chose to become a lawyer in the first place? —you know, that sort of thing," he exampled.

"He even told me about the old-school practice of offering to write a will for free, as a retirement plan. 'You see, you might not get much

for setting them up in the beginning,' he explained, 'but when they pass away, everything they've accumulated has to be either liquidated or retitled to someone else. That is where the money is, and you get a percentage of it all. The only thing is, though, you have to outlive your clients to cash in,' he satirically noted. I actually found him to be quite interesting," Norman remarked.

"It is interesting," Bo thoughtfully concurred.

"Makes you think, doesn't it?" Norman rhetorically proposed. "Well, I guess I'd better start out by saying that he always thought of himself as being a fair judge, and then, most importantly, an honorable man. Now, even though he was an affable man, he took the gravity of his decisions very seriously. He never was that kind of pontificating judge that degraded the offender if he had to hand down a harsh sentence. He was the kind of judge who held that the sentence itself was the judgement, and he separated his personal views as to the immorality or indecency of the offender's act. This naturally made him one of the more popular judges with the voters, for he was seen as a fair judge, one who not only applied the law as required, but did it as compassionately as possible."

"Just the same, I have to tell you, as much as he outwardly presented himself as a good-natured and content man, this was hardly the case. He was really quite a tortured man, and it all began with this insurance lawsuit I was helping him with. It was gnawing at his soul, and the longer the case went on, the greater his inner struggle began to take its toll. So his suffering went on, and for as long as the insurance company refused to give him back his life's savings, his torment continued.

"At first I thought that the seeds of his consternation were simply over the loss of his money, but actually, I couldn't have been further from the truth. For over a year and a half, he filed motion after motion as the insurance company responded in kind. Finally, in a great moment of exasperation on one dreary Friday afternoon, a day I will never forget, he chose to confide in me the real reason why he was obviously writhing agony.

"He had just signed another motion to be filed, and in a total fit of disgust, threw down his pen, sighed heavily, and reclined back in his large leather chair. 'For the rest of your life,' I then heard him mutter under his breath while looking down and slowly shaking his head, only to repeat, 'For the rest of your life,' a second time."

"Are you feeling alright?" I asked.

"Yes, I'm okay," the judge answered, but he didn't look up.

"Are you sure?" I said to him.

"Yes, I'm okay," the judge repeated, in finally raising his head. "Well, it's Friday afternoon. Do you have anything planned for tonight? I mean, are you in a hurry to go somewhere, or do you have a moment?" the judge asked.

"No, no place in particular, Judge," I told him. "What do you need?" I asked.

"Well, if you do have a moment, I just thought I'd tell you why I've been so damn aggravated with this case, that's all," he said in frustration, only to add in a much softer tone, "That is of course, if you have time."

"Sure," I told him. "I have all the time in the world."

"You see, I knew that something was bothering him all along, and I knew it wasn't just over the money. I felt that he was now actually reaching out to talk to somebody about it, and that someone was me, — but God knows, for what reason, I have no idea. So, there he was, telling me almost repentantly, 'I have always tried to be a decent man. For over twenty years I served on the bench and I have always considered myself a good judge. The first time you are elected you say to yourself, you are lucky, but after you win a second time, you almost begin to feel that you were meant to be there. Then, after that, I think that a sort of arrogance comes over you. Now, I don't believe it is a conscious thing. That would be reprehensible. No, I think that it rather creeps up on you. I think it's more like Shakespeare so aptly put, — it's more pernicious than a summer-seeming lust,' he paraphrased.

"It was then that I commented, 'I guess this metamorphosis is actually a job hazard, isn't it?' just trying to lighten things up a bit."

"It's more than that," the judge seriously replied. "It's a sin. It's nothing more than the sin of pride. One of the worst of all," he asserted like a condemned man with absolutely no chance of reprieve. "You see, I always believed in, and unequivocally supported, the statutes of limitations," he said. "Many a time a person would file their complaint late and I would deny them their just day in court because the statutes of limitations had run out for them. It was simply too late for them to file, according to the law. It didn't matter what the case was about, the statutes were the statutes, and that was that, as far as I was concerned," he said emphatically.

"I even remember when it was obvious one time that this person was irreparably harmed, —and I mean irreparably," he stressed, "but I still held up the statutory limitation," he maintained. "I told him that my time was valuable, and that if he had not taken his time seriously, that was his problem. And even though he claimed he did not know that he could seek some relief through the court at the time, I still denied him. It was then he said something to me that I never forgot," he explicitly gestured with his index finger, as I should never forget as well.

"He told me that," the judge continued, 'if a man goes into a barber shop and comes out with a bad haircut, he gets over it. It grows out and he still remains who he is, —but the barber has to live with the reputation of being a bad barber for the rest of his life. So, for the rest of your life, you will have to live with the fact that you are a bad judge. You know it is morally wrong to do what you have done to me today, and mark my word, you will pay for it, judge. And pay for it you will, —for the rest of your life!'"

"Now, I have to tell you," the judge then went on to reveal, "I, myself, did not find out how I had been wronged until about two weeks before the statutes of limitations would have applied to my own situation. If

I hadn't been a judge and knew how to file the paperwork myself, we wouldn't be here today," he conceded. "And so you know, at this point, it isn't about the money at all, it's about all those people I let suffer because I denied them their day in court. And for what? Because I was so important? Because I was the great judge? Because my time was more valuable than theirs?" he paused for a moment. "And so, you have to understand now, it isn't only about that one particular guy who cursed me. The way I see it, no matter how much I wronged him, it's also about all the other people that I scarred in the name of justice, too, —knowing full well, as human beings, they deserved better," he shamefully stated. "Oh, for the rest of my life," he repeated, as once again he hung his head low in disgrace, this time with his face in his hands. It was so sad to watch, and why he told me this story, I will never know, but it sure made me feel bad for the guy," Norman solemnly acknowledged.

"Yeah, I guess it's always different when the shoe is on the other foot, isn't it?" Bo remarked, in a tone that was not so sympathetic.

"You can say that again," Norman agreed. "But you still haven't heard the end of it yet," he taunted.

"Oh yeah? What else is there?" Bo questioned in renewed interest.

"Well, after all that fighting went on with the insurance company for almost two years, they finally agreed to settle. The only thing that remained was that the settlement terms were reached around Christmas time, and since no judge wants to work then, the final hearing was put off until after the first week in January," Norman further related.

"So, he won, then?" Bo expressly questioned.

"Let's just say he found the peace he was looking for," Norman said.

"So, how much money did he get, anyway?" Bo persisted.

"Why, he didn't get any money whatsoever," Norman declaratively stated. "He dropped dead two days before the settlement was actually signed. He got adjudicated by God, —that's what he got," Norman historically determined.

"Which also goes to show you," Bo supplemented, "that you really can't be cursed by someone else. You can only be cursed by your own hand, —and only redeemed by the hand of God," he empathetically stipulated.

Catch-As-Catch-Can

Fred Smith, like so many others who had settled in the small town, got there because his point of discharge was from the military base nearby. He was an average man in his late-forties who wore his graying hair cut close, as all career military men seemed to do, even after retirement. He was also someone who was so pedestrian that although he had become a regular he went virtually unnoticed, taking a seat at the end of the counter every day at about three o'clock in the afternoon.

Fred was so mundane that if he had been cast in a movie, he would have been either the third man in line at the local hardware store or the person walking his mongrel dog across the street. He most assuredly would not have gotten a line. He was neither tall, nor short, fat nor thin, he was just there. It would be quite the metaphor to say that every after afternoon he would plant himself down at the end of the counter to be watered, for even more unnoteworthy, he was the embodiment of the perennial plant which had never flowered.

Mild-mannered in every way, from his soft-spoken tenor to his slow and unremarkable gait, he was also the epitome of stealth. On one hand, he might have not been the life of the party, but on the other he was always invited, for he couldn't offend a fly and was always quite pleasant to be around. Fred was an observer, a studier of the human condition, and not just a member of the cast. Naturally, this trait fit right in with his titled duties of having been a Veterinary Food Inspector for the US Army, having been in charge of overseeing practically everything that the base had to procure for its foodstuffs.

Bo, the owner of the restaurant, thoroughly enjoyed Fred, for he always found Fred's analytical observations to be very interesting and well thought out. These conversations were also, both in their timing and content, a pleasant afternoon diversion for the hard working

restauranteur. As far as Fred was concerned, his visits were also an enjoyable experience because he not only had someone to listen to his ruminations, but it capped off his usual day of fishing in a most gratifying way. At least three times a week, Fred would get up and out the door about seven in the morning and take his motorized john boat to one of the many local lakes to see what he could catch. This he did by himself, and therefore by the end of his excursion he consequently found himself wanting for some company, or someone at least to share his thoughts with.

"So, how'd it go today?" Bo asked on one Wednesday afternoon, personally drawing Fred his usual beer.

"Caught a couple specks," Fred plainly reported.

"You know Fred, I'll tell you what I'll do for you; if you give me those two specks, I'll pan fry them you for dinner tomorrow night. Thursdays aren't usually all that busy, and I don't think you've ever been in here at night. It's nothing like it is in the day. Also, it's on the house, too. I mean, you come in here often enough, and you never try to pester me for free beer like everyone else does, so I think that's the least I can do. Besides, it's your fish anyway," Bo noted.

"Well, I guess that could be okay," Fred slowly answered, after thinking about the offer for a moment. "I don't usually go out at night," he added, pausing for yet another second, "but I think that would be alright," he finally affirmed. "Now I don't mind paying, Bo. You deserve something for frying them up," he stated respectfully.

"Oh, don't be ridiculous, Fred. Like I said, it's your fish anyway. And besides, I look at you as a friend, not just as a customer," Bo said sincerely. "If you want to, the next time you catch more that you can eat, just give me some, that's all, — if you still want to do something. Other than that, I'll see you tomorrow night about seven, okay?"

"Yeah, I can be here about seven," Fred evenly replied.

"Good, then seven it is," Bo certifiably established.

And as reliable as one can be, Fred made his first foray into the evening world of Charlie's Restaurant. To be sure, the evening crowd was nothing like the lunch crowd, and especially not the afternoon crowd either, which usually consisted of only two or three people at a time, besides Fred. This was a whole new existence to him. There were people eating in the booths, there were people playing the juke box, and there were people laughing festively, but most uncomfortable to Fred was that the counter where he normally sat alone was all but full. Luckily, however, the one seat that he usually occupied at the far end of the counter was still vacant, and as unobtrusively as possible he meandered over to it and sat down.

"So, I see you made it, Fred," Bo greeted after he had personally gone to the end of the counter where Fred had taken up his usual position.

"Yeah, I'm here," Fred replied in a manifest manner.

"Well, I'll start your dinner now, and I'll have Regis wait on you," Bo said accommodatingly. "Regis, give Fred here anything he wants. You can make a ticket out, but make sure give it to me, not him" he directed.

"Okay," Regis said with a simple smile, with Bo passing her by on his way to the kitchen.

"So, your name is Fred, then?" Regis asked, once arriving at the far end of the the counter.

"Yes," Fred replied.

"Well, Fred, what do you want? I can't it get for you if you don't tell me," Regis coaxed.

"Oh, just a draft," Fred replied straightforwardly.

"Okay, Fred, here it is," Regis presented, putting down the pilsner glass of beer upon a cardboard coaster before the unassuming man.

"So, I have a second," Regis advanced, "What brought you in here tonight? I've never seen you in here before. And how do you know Bo, anyway?" she asked in succession, trying her best to make the obviously reserved man feel at home.

"I've only been in here in the afternoon," Fred responded factually. "Usually it's Betty who waits on me, and sometimes Bo, but that's all," he answered with no further elaboration.

"Well, Fred," Regis again addressed him specifically, "Now that you are here, it will be me who will be waiting on you. And, I expect you to have a good time, too. That is why you came in here tonight, wasn't it? —to have a good time?" she alluringly proposed.

"Actually, I came in here because I gave Bo some fish I caught and he offered to fry them up for me. That's why I am here," he blandly explained.

"And to visit me, right?" Regis challenged directly with a smile.

"Eh,—I guess so. I guess you could say that, if you want too," he responded as politely as he could.

An awakening now began in Fred to which he had never experienced before. It was the concept of frivolity that now came tauntingly to invade his otherwise conservative nature. It was as if a battle had begun between Fred's instinctive proclivity to be cautious and, at the same time, satisfy his natural sense of curiosity. It was not that this conflict hadn't been fought before. Previously however, it was never on a social basis where it would affect him directly. His propensity "to know" had heretofore been limited to confronting the fairness and objectivity of enforcing a military dictate to which he felt might be applied in an unfair manner. However, regardless of the outcome of these conflicts, it still remained in the particular that he had no skin in the game, either way.

This time it was totally different. This time, his decision process concerned his personal welfare, to engage in, or not, as the case might be, a lifestyle to which he was totally unfamiliar with, throwing caution to the wind and having no alternative plan as to the consequences that his actions might bring. Fred full well accepted that he and he alone was responsible for his social conduct. Nonetheless, with apprehension aside, and after finishing his meal, he concluded that he would indeed return to this new realm of humanity, —even if it was only for observational purposes.

It was then that Fred had become a regular Friday night customer. Sometimes he ate, but moreover he only came in desiring to become "a part of it all." He was surprised that so many of the younger folks who would sit next to him would actually befriend him on an intimate nature. Vietnam was over and no one seemed to have the slightest intention of doing anything more than simply "living for today." Everyone, which now included Fred, was welcomed to engage. For the most part, it was the unabashed "liberated" young girls that took him by surprise, and the more he came in, the more he wished the women of his own generation were like them. He coveted the free and unfettered spirit that this "younger generation" represented, and began to crave having a woman with the same unbridled passion. Boldly, he then decided to actually do something about it, for now he rationalized to himself that he, like everyone else, should at least try to have one of his dreams come true.

"I don't know if you know what I did in the service, Bo, but I was basically a meat inspector," Fred began one Friday afternoon after coming back from fishing.

"Really?" Bo reacted in surprise, for Fred had never mentioned this commonality this before.

"Well, that was one of my jobs," Fred redefined. "Actually, I was what they define as a Veterinary Food Inspection Specialist. Basically, I was in charge of inspecting all the food that came onto the base, how it was packaged, how it was stored, and primarily, checking to see if what was purchased was actually the item that was ordered.

"You know, Fred, that's a pretty responsible position to have, isn't it?" Bo rhetorically complemented.

"I always took it seriously," Fred responded in a deadpan manner. "Why there was one time that one of the meat companies wanted me to overlook the fact they me sent a lower grade of meat than the specs required, and offered me a whole side of beef to ignore it, too. Now, it wasn't the guy who made me the offer that offended me, because I see that kind of stuff go on all the time. And I'm not a prude, either. — but simply, I just couldn't do it. It was the soldiers' food. They at least deserve to be fed well. After all, they don't get paid that much, and they put their lives on the line. As far as I'm concerned, they deserve a good meal, and it isn't going to be me to keep them from getting it. That's all," he dismissed with conviction.

"I'm with you Fred," Bo agreed without further elaboration.

"Anyway, I can tell you another one, too, —that is, if you want to hear it," Fred genially offered.

"Sure, go ahead. I got time," Bo responded.

"Well, because I had this reputation for being a regular guy, and one who always told it like it was, too, this new Lieutenant came to me and said, 'You know, Fred, since everyone around here trusts you and I see you get along with most everybody, I'd like to get a favor from you.' Then, after I asked him exactly what he wanted, he said, 'First of all, it has come to my attention that we are having a problem with the soldiers smoking marijuana. Now, for some reason, I have been ordered to do some kind of investigation to find out exactly to what extent this has

become a problem here on the base, and so I thought that you might be able to help me?' Then I said, 'What can I do?' Then he said, 'What I need is a good pair of eyes and ears, that's about all. Someone who can give me at least some kind of idea of what is actually going on around here. You know no one is going to tell me anything, but regardless, I still have to fill out some kind of report. You of all people know that,' he pointed out.

"So, I did think about it for a second, but then I told him, 'Sir, I would like to help you, but I wouldn't know what marijuana looked like if I tripped over a whole bale of it.' Then he said, 'You don't have to see anything. All you have to do is smell it. That would be good enough. At least it will give me some place to start, Sergeant.'"

"Then I informed him that I didn't even know what it smelled like, either. Well, he had an answer for that one, too. And then said this, something I never forgot, 'You don't have to worry about that, because once you do smell it, you will never forget the smell. There is nothing else like it. So then, I take it if you do smell anything strange, you will report it to me, will you not, Sargent?' he more or less ordered. 'Yes, sir, of course,' I told him."

"But, I really wasn't going to do anything of the kind," Fred admitted. "You see, first of all it wasn't in my job description to investigate the other people that I worked with. My only job was to investigate if the food on the base was properly ordered, accounted for, and stored. Second of all, I'm not a rat,—that, to me, was the most important thing. I would never rat out somebody for something like that," he staunchly declared, reposing back in his seat to clearly observe Bo's reaction to his final statement.

Chuckling in amusement, Bo responded, "Fred, if you want me to find someone who will give you a joint, why don't you just ask me?

"The thing is, Bo, I never did anything like this before," Fred sheepishly conceded. "But, I see all these people at night having a good time, and all I could think about is what that lieutenant said. I just can't help but be curious," he candidly confessed.

"Aw, don't worry Fred. When you come in tonight, I'll tell somebody to give you one, that's all. I'll have one of the girls who smoke that stuff just give it to you, too. Now, this of course, is not going to happen in here. You know that, don't you?" Bo firmly stressed.

"I understand," Fred acknowledged.

"When she comes over to you, she will ask you if you want to go outside, and all you have to do is go with her," Bo instructed casually. "Then, what goes on after you leave here, is nothing of my concern, — and I mean that. I am a restaurant and bar owner. I am not a drug dealer, —and I am not a pimp, either," he delineated with a slight grin. "Now, I have to get back in the kitchen and set up for tonight. And I wish you luck, Fred," he said in retreating to the kitchen.

That Friday evening was a busy one, and because Bo's full attention was relegated to his kitchen duties, he never had gotten opportunity to see if Fred had been successful in his endeavors or not. In fact, he had never gotten to see if Fred had come in at all. Regis did however, confirm at closing time that Fred indeed had come in, sat down in his usual place at the counter, ordered a draught, and before he had it finished, left with Ria. "And he never did come back," Regis quipped in a tickled manner.

It wasn't until Wednesday that Fred returned with his john boat still hitched to the back of his jeep, parking in the far corner of the parking lot, as usual. Again, it was about three in the afternoon, and since Bo had pardoned the time to listen to what he termed the "The Adventures of Fisherman Fred," he was only too ready in awaiting the angler's appearance. Finally, once seeing Fred come in the front door of the restaurant, as scheduled, the smile of good fortune panned across his face.

"Well, well, my good man, is it going to be the usual for you?" Bo greeted chipperly, after Fred had closed the door behind him.

"Yeah, I'll have one," replied Fred, taking his official place at the counter.

"So, catch anything today?" Bo asked, going over to the beer tap.

"Yeah, it was a good day. I caught a half-a-dozen small brim, and I also caught about a sixteen inch bass too," Fred reported with practically no emotion at all.

"So, wasn't that a pretty good catch?" Bo questioned, wondering why Fred wasn't more excited.

"Oh, it's a pretty good catch, alright," Fred benignly agreed. "But that isn't what I'm disappointed about," he revealed somberly.

"So what's the problem, Fred? Didn't you get what you wanted last Friday?" Bo asked in concern.

"Yeah, I got it," he acknowledged tepidly. "But that isn't the problem," he said in a complaining tone. "It didn't do anything for me. I went home and smoked half of it, and it only put me asleep. I don't see how all these people can say it's so great. I was hoping that I would feel something, —but nothing, nothing at all. Like I said, all it did was just put me to sleep," he testified in total disappointment.

"You know, you have to understand, Fred, it effects everybody different, no different than beer. Now when it comes to beer," Bo began specifically, "some people get rowdy, some get to crying in their beer. Then, there are some like you, who can drink one or two and simply leave it at that, while others will drink until they almost pass out. Nobody's the same," he annotated in fact.

"I guess you're right," Fred said in acceptance.

"Sure I'm right, Fred," Bo reasserted. "But I will tell you one thing though," he further offered, "and that is that you can pretty much tell what kind of person a beer drinker is, just by the brand they drink," he proposed.

"Really?" responded Fred in interest.

"Oh, yeah," Bo said flatly. "For example, if you drink Schlitz, you probably have the tendency to be a redneck, if you drink Budweiser, you are a partier, Coors, you think you're a Yuppie, and if you order a Heineken, you're trying for that intellectual European look. Now, it's probably not that way all the time, but you have to admit, there is a degree of truth to it," Bo grinned in looking for some support to his thesis.

"I never thought about it before, but then again, I'm not in the beer business. I guess it could be seen that way," Fred tenuously agreed.

"Anyway, my point is Fred, everything, including pot, affects everyone different. Maybe it's just not for you, so don't worry about it," he consoled.

"Maybe not, I guess," Fred finally conceded, still looking a tad dejected.

Nothing more was mentioned about Fred's brief encounter with his attempt to capture up the passions of the modern day era until about two weeks later when Fred practically burst through the front door in a most untypical state of haste, making a direct bee-line to his usual haunt at the counter.

"I'll have a draft, Betty," Fred announced, even before taking his seat. "Ask Bo if he has a second, too, would you?"

"Sure, Fred," she answered, "What'd you do, catch a whale?" Betty joked in seeing his exuberance.

"Oh no, nothing like that. But would you just ask Bo if I could see him for a second?" he politely requested again, casting a sense of extreme importance.

"Sure," Betty replied. "Here you go," she said, putting down his drink. "I'll go get him for you," she succinctly noted, leaving to go to the kitchen.

"Hey, Fred, how's it going?" Bo greeted, once he had gotten to where Fred was seated.

"You won't believe it. Wait till I tell you what happened," Fred said in restraint, as if not to be heard by Betty, who had gone over to the other side of the room to clear off and reset a table.

"So, go on, tell me," Bo urged in interest.

"You remember I told you that after only smoking half of that marijuana cigarette I had gotten from Ria, that I just fell asleep a couple of Fridays ago?" he asked.

"Yeah, I remember," Bo confirmed.

"Well, just so you know, I also go over to the NCO Club besides here, about once a week, —have been for years," he disclosed matter-of-factly.

"So?" Bo replied with unconcern.

"Well, anyway, last Thursday, when I went there, I told the bar maid, her name is Joanie, all about me trying the pot and what happened. Then, after I finished, she went and asked me what I did with the other half of the cigarette I had left. When I told her that I still had it, she then asked me if she came over to my place, could she have it?"

"Of course I said sure, because I had no intention of using it," he asided. Anyway, to make a long story short, she smoked the darn thing and then she attacked me! Bo, I've got to tell you, I never had such wild sex before in all my life! It was unreal! She kept me up the entire night after that," he testified in a low tone of hushed amazement, not wanting Betty to hear him.

"Oh, you old sex dog, you," Bo chuckled wryly.

"No, I'm not kidding you," Fred said in all seriousness.

"I'm sure you're not," Bo responded in kind.

"So, —" Fred paused for a moment, "Do you think that Ria will be coming in on Friday?" he then asked sheepishly.

"I don't know, Fred. She comes in a number of times a week. If you want, you can give me your phone number and tell me when you will normally be home, and I'll give it to her when comes in next. That's all I can say," Bo offered with a helping attitude.

"I can do that," Fred responded without hesitation, "Got a piece of paper?"

Then, for Bo, it became a mystery without any clues, for Fred did not return again for over a month –and neither did Ria. It was as if the both of them had fallen off the face of the earth. Then, on one Thursday afternoon at about two thirty, Fred unexpectedly came rushing in through the back kitchen door in a complete panic.

"You didn't see Joanie come in here, did you, Bo? Oh, excuse me," he interrupted himself. "Sorry about coming in the back door."

"That's okay, Fred," Bo dismissed, putting down the knife in his hand. "Where have you been? I haven't seen you in a month," he first questioned in interest.

"I been home, that's all. So, you haven't seen Joanie then, today, have you?" he anxiously repeated his original question.

"No, Fred, I haven't. All you told me once, was that she worked at the NCO Club. I never met her," Bo declared, rhetorically adding, "How would I even know what she looks like?"

"Oh, yeah, that's right," Fred commented in befuddlement, looking up and away for a moment. "Well, have you seen Ria, then?" he asked directly.

"Nope, haven't seen her either, not since I saw you last, in fact," Bo testified.

"Well, just the same, I came to say goodbye and I really won't be back," Fred announced, whereas Bo took the news in utter surprise.

"You can't tell me what happened?" Bo solicited in raising his eyebrows.

"Oh, I guess I could. I got the boat parked out back so they don't see it," Fred said, going over to the back door and looking out to check on the boat's existence. "Okay, I guess I got a few minutes," he said in a brief reprieve from his paranoia. "You see, after you gave Ria my phone number, she called and I made a date for her to come over with some more marijuana. I also made the date so that Joanie could be there, because it was she who really wanted it.

"All that was fine, but then, after they both got stoned, the two of them went and attacked me together," Fred continued. "If I thought that Joanie was the wildest thing that ever happened to me, it was nothing compared to that," he exclaimed. "At first I thought I was in heaven, —you know, living every man's dream, being the king of Siam. But let me tell you, at best, it lasted a week," he declared. "They never left me alone. It was sex, sex, sex, all the time. And If it wasn't sex, it was getting more stoned. And then it was sending me to the PX to go shopping for them. I, —I can't take it anymore! I just can't take it anymore, Bo!" he stammered, almost to the point of convulsion.

"Take it easy, Fred, take it easy," Bo comforted slowly, trying to calm the situation.

"Okay, okay, I got it," Fred said, finally regaining his composure after taking a deep breath. "Well, I just want you to know that you're a great guy before I take off. I got everything that's important to me already packed up, and I got my boat. I managed to sneak out about an hour ago without waking them up. So, I guess I am off," he concluded, putting his hand out to shake.

"It was great to know you, Fred, but still, if you are ever in the area again, don't hesitate to stop by, even if you have to sneak in the back door," Bo added with a warm smile.

"I will if I can," Fred replied, turning to let himself out. "Oh, and by the way," he called back with the door half-open, "I just want you to know, for the record, —it's easier to catch a fish than it is to catch a dream!"

The Deacon

William Thornton Boutin was from Louisiana and the son a hard working welder who made his living on the docks of New Orleans. Having been raised in one of the outlying towns that was the better part of an hour away by car, his nature reflected nothing of the frivolous and provocative behavior that the city folks were famed for. His mother had seven children with no complaint and was the daughter of one of the local preachers who was known for his hellfire and brimstone sermons. William was the middle child, and had an independence about him that his other siblings did not.

The mother took the children to church on a regular basis and the father went on the religious holidays, including never having missed the mother's day sermon. For the most part, however, the father stayed home on Sundays to effect the maintenance of their almost one hundred year old home. The family's heritage was a long one, and the plentitude of its extended members lived throughout the parish. This caused the preacher of their church to be a very busy man in trying to attend to everyone's salvation, not only spiritually, but as the mortal patriarch of the clan as well, for he was also the mother's father.

Although the blistering sermons from the pastor were a thing to behold while his flock attended the services, once outside of its walls he became more of counselor at large than a rebuker. Preacher Prudhomme, as was his moniker, had always had a fondness for William, and without any pretenses hoped that his grandson would someday follow in his footsteps. Besides the gospel, the grandfather would constantly try to engrain upon his intended successor the importance of his heritage and one's sacred duty to have it honored.

When William was a young boy he was allowed to stay with his grandfather after the Sunday church services to help with the small church's cleaning, and otherwise keep his grandfather company. Because

there were no other replacements on the horizon to remarry the strict preacher after his wife had passed away in birthing his only daughter, it was thought that the companionship of the boy would "do him good."

The first thing that was taught to the young boy was that his grandfather was not "Paw Paw," was not "Grandpa," and he was certainly not to be called "Pops." He was to be called "Grandfather," and that was the extent of it. In turn, there never existed such a person called Billy either. His grandfather called him William and was never heard to call him anything else. 'Bill' could be accepted from others in the vernacular sense by the strict disciplinarian, but whenever he heard someone refer to his grandson as "Willie," or especially "Little Willie," the offence by no means went uncorrected.

Bill took his melioration seriously, and by the time he was sixteen he learned the strength of silence whenever listening to the outreach of others. This was particularly effective when exposed to the wants and desires of the insecure young girls who came to the Wednesday night prayer meetings. This was his world and all was copasetic until he lost the favors of his most treasured conquest, Trinity Dupre. Bill had often taken Trinity to the local movie theatre, the school's football games, and other such public events to such a degree that he had self-righteously assumed that she was under his exclusive dominion.

Henry Huet, on the other hand, was under no such illusion when he handed Trinity a written invitation to the senior prom which she thereupon happily accepted. Henry's family had lived in the Parish for as long as Bill's had and was just as revered in every way except for one thing, —they had a lot more money. Sugar cane was king to the Huets, and Trinity was now going to the prom in style.

Mortified, Bill's entire self-esteem had been crushed as his arrogance took over his otherwise imperturbable behavior. He felt humiliated in the only world he had ever known and only hoped that somehow he could escape. But to where? was his problem.

"Well, Bodie, I'll be graduating in a couple of weeks. Know of any work around here I can get?" Bill asked one of his father's weekend fishing buddies who was busily cleaning the day's catch, out on the back porch. "I'll be needin' a full time job," he added.

"Not 'round cheer, son," Bodie replied, cutting the head off a redfish. "But there is a fella I know of who is lookin' for a guy to go on the road, —ifin' you're interested, that is," he answered with little concern.

"Oh yeah? What's it doin'? Bill questioned further.

"They put them guard rails up along the sides of the interstate. They go all over the place," Bodie said, continuing to gut the fish.

"Can you get me the guy's number?" Bill asked.

"Sure, I'll git it for you on Monday, and drop it by on the way home," Bodie told the boy, now beginning to scale what was left of the fish.

The Interstate Guardrail Company was happy to employ the six foot strapping young man. He spoke little, earned his money, and did what he was told. The crew itself also worked hard, and on a regular basis after quitting time would usually all together find a small local place to grab a beer or two, before heading off to the motel they were temporarily lodged.

It was on a late summer afternoon, when the entire guardrail crew came into Charlie's Restaurant, practically taking up all of the counter space that the place had to offer. Not quite five o'clock yet, it was still eighty five degrees outside when they had knocked off early because of the heat.

"Y'all got a cold Budweiser back there?" the big burly crew chief was the first to ask after everyone had taken a seat.

"Sure do," answered Regis, the waitress behind the counter, turning around and sliding open the top of the beer cooler. "Here you go," she replied pleasantly, putting down the long neck bottle, followed by placing a pilsner glass atop a cardboard coaster.

"So what'll be for the rest of you?" Regis unspecifically asked, to then attend to the rest of the crew's requests.

Regis had been raised in California until her second year in high school when her father was transferred to the military base nearby. She had an airy, pleasant attitude with no discernable ambition other than to enjoy life. She fashioned herself the elemental California girl, naturally in tune with life itself, and her demeanor was as care free as a summer's breeze. She did save her money though, and managed to buy a classic 1959 Chevy convertible, which was her prize possession and statement to the world of who she was.

Bill had never met such a creature before, so much different from the girls that he was used to, and this fascinated him. After about a week, the entire crew had blended right in with the locals. And while their initial reason to come was only to have a beer and get out of the heat, they began to eat their dinner there as well. This development caused most of them now to gravitate to one of the corner booths when they came, yielding to the more comfortable seating. But Bill never did, preferring to still sit at the counter by himself where Regis was assigned to work, only ever ordering a beer.

"They call me Deacon, by the way," he introduced himself the first time Bill had the chance to introduce himself to the cheery-tempered sprite of a girl.

"I never knew a 'Deacon' before," Regis replied, "How'd you get that name?" she asked in a clueless fashion.

"My Grandfather was a preacher, and since I used to help him a lot at the church, everyone called me 'The Little Deacon.' After a while, the 'Little' fell off, but the 'Deacon' stayed," he casually explained.

"So, where are you from?" Regis asked, half in interest, and half because it was part of her job.

"Loosianna, 'bout an hour from N'Orlins," Deacon answered shortly. "How 'bout you?" he asked in return.

"I'm from California, can't you tell?" she said leadingly, flipping her light blond hair back with an alluring effect.

"I never knew anyone from California before," Bo plainly stated.

"Well, here I am," Regis stated flirtatiously. "I never knew anyone from Louisiana either," she responded with a smile.

"It's a lot better than being from here, I can tell you that," Deacon responded.

"Oh, I kind of like it," Regis responded. "People aren't so much in a hurry here, and the rent's cheap, too," she offered affably.

"Yeah, but there ain't nothin' to do. Ain't got no bayous to go fishin' in, ain't got no good party places to go to at night that's got any good music, —and the food here ain't worth eatin', either," Deacon responded bluntly.

"Oh, the food here is good," Regis testified congenially.

"Got any crawfish?" Deacon asked directly.

"No, I don't even know what they are," Regis answered unpretentiously.

"See, that's what I mean. Y'all don't even know how to eat here," Deacon said dismissively, taking another drink from his beer.

For the next few weeks it was always the same. In came the whole crew and sat themselves in the corner booth, ordering something to eat, while Deacon sat at the counter by himself, incessantly degrading the small town while at the same time bragging about his beloved home, "Loosianna." He never ordered anything to eat, and one evening Bo himself asked the young construction worker why. "Because you ain't got no shrimp creole. You ain't got no jambalaya. Why, you ain't even got any shrimp heads to suck," Deacon all but chastised the owner out loud. Hesitant to start a direct confrontation in front of the other customers, Bo decided the better way to handle the rude remark was to simply accept the statement for who said it, only to respond, "Okay," and retreat back into the kitchen.

Nonetheless, Deacon's persistent negative comments about each and every thing in the entire town, began to annoy Bo. The restaurant had always had a pleasant atmosphere, and having received numerous compliments on his bill of fare, Bo was proud of his accomplishments. Thus, in trying to understand why anyone would behave in such an insulting manner, he decided one evening to question some of the others in the work crew after Deacon had left early, completely by himself.

"First of all, you need to know the real reason why he's called "Deacon," one of the older men of the crew began from the corner booth. "We gave him that name," he declared with a wry smile. "Now, that whole business of him helping out his grandfather the preacher when he was young, is true enough, —but that's not how he got his name," he stated correctively. "We gave it to him because the first place he looks to find when we come into a new town, is a small church that has a Wednesday night prayer meeting, just so he can pick up one of the girls there, —that's why."

"Well, yesterday was Wednesday and he was here until we closed at ten," Bo factually stated.

"That's only cause he's trying to get Regis over there to go out with him, that's all," the crew chief spoke up. "That's the only reason he does anything, is to pick up some cooter," he grinned, as the other fellows in the crew chuckled at the truth. "And I'll tell you somethin' else, he ain't gonna be ordering anything to eat 'round here either. No Sir, ole Deacon's tighter than Dick's hat band," he euphemistically declared. "He buys a loaf of bread at the grocery store and eats bologna sandwiches in his room. He saves every cent he gets. I bet you he never ordered anything more than the cheapest draft you sell. And I'll also bet you he never left more than the change for a tip, too. Ain't that right?" he questioned.

"Yeah, I believe that's right," Bo agreed, slightly shaking his head. "Well, fellas, all I can tell you all that I certainly do appreciate your business, so your next beer is on me, okay?" he offered in appreciation.

"Well, we like comin' in here, too. And thank you very much," the crew chief replied accordingly.

"Yeah, thanks a lot, Bo," another of the group spoke up, followed by everyone else at the table.

It was on the following Monday night, about six o'clock, that Bo noticed Deacon was actually ramping up his usual disparaging comments, but this time the special of the day was included, commenting "it wasn't fit to eat."

"What was the problem with The Deacon tonight?" Bo asked Regis after the restaurant had closed for the evening.

"Oh, I went out with him after work on Saturday, and I guess when he didn't get what he wanted, so he just got mean, that's all," Regis replied indifferently, continuing to wipe down the counter. "Besides, going to Eve's Oyster Bar isn't my idea of a having a good time, and I told him so," she expounded apathetically.

"So you don't like Eve's?" Bo commented satirically.

"I hate oysters! They are so slimy," Regis said in disgust, giving up a small shudder with a sour face and sticking her tongue out.

"Well, you know what I told you when you started here," Bo authoritatively began, "If you go out with a customer and you compromise yourself, he's not going to leave you a tip anymore. And also, if you don't, —he damn sure won't leave you anything, either. But like I said, you're an adult and I'm not going to tell you what to do with your social life. Nevertheless, if you keep going out with the customers, you can expect it to cost you, —and when it does, don't come crying to me when you need make more money," he warned in all seriousness.

"All he ever left me was the change, anyway," Regis responded with a shrug.

Thereafter, as Regis began paying less attention to Deacon, and more to the other suitors that sat on the counter, he became even more imperiously pugnacious in his general demeanor. This did not escape

anyone. Thereupon, in an attempt to quell the discordance that Deacon was creating, Bo decided to make some red beans and rice, "N'Orlins" style, hoping that this gesture would soften the atmosphere.

After ordering all the necessary ingredients, Bo started this project on a Wednesday, figuring to have it ready to be served by Friday night when the entire crew usually stopped by for dinner. After letting the beans soak overnight, by Thursday morning he was ready to add the rest of the ingredients before letting the entire brew cook slowly for the rest of the day. Finally, by the time the evening had come around, Bo noticed that even though the taste he was seeking to achieve was absolutely perfect, the mixture was still too soupy. He thereupon decided that it would congeal together more once it was refrigerated, and consequently put the lid on the large five gallon cauldron and placed it in the walk-in.

Disappointingly however, by the next morning the concoction's consistency had not changed to any noticeable degree. Something had to be done. The cuisine had to be perfect. And although many in the restaurant industry are of the opinion that since their recipes are flawless, if an undesired result occurs, any attempt to correct it thereafter, is simply impossible. Thereupon, the entirety of it all should be disposed of, and the project be restarted from the beginning. Bo was by no means a believer in this school of thought. He always listened intently to anyone who had something new to offer and took the advice gratefully, feeling that even if he did not have a use for it in the present, it still might be of some value later. It was with this in mind, that he recalled a lesson that that was given to him years before, which perhaps was now the answer to his current predicament.

"If ever you got a sauce that's too thin, —whether it be beef stew, or oxtail soup like this, makes no difference. And you got the flavor juuuust right, —and don't want to change it in any way, other than to get it thicker? This is what you do," an elderly black cook told Bo in the restaurant he had worked in while still in high school. "All you gots to

do is take a handful of rice, put it in this here piece of cheesecloth, tie it up with some of this string we use to truss up the roasts with, and then just throw it into the pot," which he did. "And there you have it!" he declared. "When the rice cooks, it'll soak up aaaall that extra juice, — and then the sauce'll do the tighten up for ya, all by itself," he certified with the smile of a man who was proud of his hard earned knowledge. "And, like I said, it won't change the flavor one darn bit," he certified in finality.

This advice Bo had never forgotten because not only did the cook's solution work exactly the way it was explained, but because he also had a great affinity for the elderly man who talked to him like a son. It was Bo's first job, and regardless of the hard work, he had always felt at home there. He also wondered, from time to time, if his first job would somehow hold the greatest influence over him for the rest his life. Nonetheless, his thoughts were now only focused on getting the red beans and rice to do the "tighten up" as he was taught.

It wasn't all that easy though, for instantly Bo realized that not only didn't he have any cheesecloth, the local purveyors didn't carry it, either. And then it hit him. He had bought a box of those new Handi Wipes that the health inspector had suggested he buy, so he didn't have to constantly bleach out the bar rags.

"You know, that just might work. And I can use a bag tie to secure it, too," Bo said to himself optimistically, feeling he had found the solution to his precarious state of affairs.

Nothing could have been more predictable that Friday evening when the crew came in. And as Regis first went over to wait on the hard working crew who had taken their customary position the corner booth, Bo specifically walked over to get Deacon his draft.

"Well, Deacon, this time I think I finally have something that I think that you actually can't resist ordering to eat," Bo said in a most congenial tone, putting down Deacon's usual draft.

"Listen, I told you before. You don't have anything in here that I would eat. You ain't even got a Po' Boy on the menu. As far as I'm concerned, everything you got on the menu is just crap. Now if some of these other folks want to eat your crap, then I say let 'em. But like I told you a thousand times, I ain'ta be eatin' any of it, Deacon said in resolve.

"No, Deacon, this time you are wrong," Bo persisted with a smile. "This time, I made something that you've got to try. And because I greatly value your opinion, seeing that you claim to be the expert here in 'Loosianna cookin,' your meal will be on the house. How's that?" Bo questioned in an upscale manner.

"Oh yeah?" You made what?" Deacon snidely replied.

"I made some red beans and rice. I even put some smoked sausage in it, too. And like I said, it's on the house. All I want is your opinion," Bo flatly petitioned.

"Red beans and rice, huh?" Deacon responded skeptically.

"That's it. Red beans and rice. And the recipe I got says, —it's the best." Bo continued with a wide smile.

"Well, okay, I'll give it a try, seein's it'll only cost me my opinion. But still, I ain't gonna be eatin' any of that other crap you sell in here," Deacon reinforced as rude as ever.

"I'll go and get you some," Bo nevertheless replied pleasantly, leaving back to the kitchen to put together a plate for his more than obnoxious guest. It was then, all of a sudden, it hit him like a rock to the side of his head. Once he had begun to stir the mixture in the large pot, as was usual before serving the mixture, he noticed that he had forgotten to take out the Handi Wipe which still contained the handful of rice. "You know something," he finally said to himself, "I've really had it with him. No matter how much I have tried to be nice to him, even though I went through all this work just to please him, he's still an insulting jerk. And I am tired of apologizing to the other customers for his nasty comments, too. He isn't even a decent person, and I really

don't even like him, either. So why am I doing this? He's just a bully, that's all. I wonder if he can take some of his own medicine?" Bo now began to entertain.

"Here it is, Deacon," Bo announced proudly, putting down the plate of food before the self-anointed Loosianna food critic.

"I guess it looks okay," deacon responded dryly, picking up his fork.

"Well, I got to go back to the kitchen now, but if you need any more, just ask Regis," Bo instructed, leaving Deacon to his own devices.

It was about a half-hour later, after Bo had caught up with the orders, he decided to go back out front and find out what Deacon had to say about his meal.

"So, what do you think?" Bo asked when he got to where Deacon was seated, noticing that the plate of food was completely eaten.

"It ain't too bad," Deacon responded, much to Bo's surprise.

"Ain't too bad?" questioned Bo in reproach.

"Yeah, that's what I said. It ain't too bad," The Deacon repeated, obviously annoyed to repeat it.

"Well, I thought it came out great," Bo challenged, "Why, I soaked the beans overnight, I put in some fresh garlic, I cut up a fresh green tomato, some okra, a couple of Vidalia onions, some celery, and then added not only some cayenne pepper, but some authentic Loosianna hot sauce as well. Then, I thought to myself, what could I possibly add to make it special? —to make it unique, just like they do in Loosianna," he eminently declared with a broad smile, dramatically pausing for a second. "I then thought that sometimes they might add some wine, but I didn't have any," he gesticulated with his palms up in the helpless admission of this fact. "Just the same," he stressed with his finger in the air, "I figured that the next best thing that I could do, was add some beer instead. So, I went over to the draft tap over there to draw some," he pointed out, "but then all of a sudden, I even got a better idea, —why not just take that old bar rag under the tap and use it? After all, that darn sure

has some flavor, I figured. And so, that's exactly what I did. I took that old bar rag and threw it right into the beans, —just like they probably do in Loosianna," Bo concluded with the proudest of grins.

"Aw, come on, I never heard of such a stupid thing," Deacon replied, totally dismissing Bo's story with a wave of his right hand.

"No sir, Deacon," Bo adamantly replied. "That's exactly what I did. That's why it tastes exactly like they make it in N'Orlins. You want to see?" Bo then offered with his eyebrows raised.

"Yeah, I wanna see," The Deacon said, standing up from the counter.

"Come on, I'll show you," Bo said, as Deacon now followed the young restaurateur in to the kitchen.

Then once the two of them had gotten aside the heavy iron stove where the five gallon kettle of red beans was still simmering away, Bo picked up the long wooden paddle that lay across the top of the pot and began to stir the spicy mixture clockwise.

"Come on, look here," Bo entreated, waving Deacon to come closer and peer directly into the pot.

It was then that Bo fished up the Handi Wipe with the rice in it and said, "See, I told you. There's the rag!" Bo decried excitedly.

And that was all she wrote for Deacon, as his eyes nearly popped out of his head. Frozen in horror, he watched red colored gravy drip down slowly from the slimy cloth and then back into the pot. He was speechless.

"See, I told you it was just like they do in N'Orlins," Bo smartly repeated his claim.

But Deacon did not respond. Still in a state of shock, he simply wandered back to his seat at the counter in total silence. And there he sat with one hand on his beer glass, not uttering a sound, not moving a muscle. Then, only a few moments later, Bo came out of the kitchen, went directly over to where the rest of the traveling construction crew was sitting, and began to retell the story of how the beans had been

prepared. Finally, when Bo had gotten to the point where he brought up the muculent beer soaked rag, the worker known as "The Deacon" just couldn't take it anymore.

"Don't eat the food! Don't eat the food here!" Deacon shrieked out as he bolted up from the counter. "I'm tellin ya, don't eat the food! It just like he said, there's a dirty rag in the beans! My God, don't eat the food in here!" he warned again, rushing over to the crew's booth while waving his hands in caution. "I saw it. He really put a dirty rag in the beans! He really did!" he exclaimed to high heaven.

Then, as a complete and utter silence fell, Deacon, realizing that he was the lone center of attention and that no one else had anything to say, stopped his ranting and just stood there in silence, waiting for anyone to make some kind of comment, —any kind of comment, but no one did.

"I think you need to go home now," Bo said in a measured tone.

Slowly, Deacon then looked about the room, and seeing that he had no followers to join him in his condemnation, he bitterly withdrew to front door, opened it smartly with left hand, turned back, looked at everyone in the room and yelled out vociferously, "Y'all can go to hell, I'm goin' back to Loosianna!"

Communion

At times there are exceptions made as to the general rules and beliefs that people impose upon themselves over what is righteous and what is not. Usually, these changes in thinking are only made after discovering that, in the grand scheme of life, they had to, only adjusting their position whenever the "unforeseen" prevailed in becoming graphically relevant. Sometimes this process is also fostered by the opposite, when it is precisely "the seen" that becomes the impetus of forcing them re-evaluate their tolerances. Didi fit exactly in this category. At only five-foot-two, she was politely referred to as a plus woman, who, by any gracious description, was so obese that it would be impossible for anyone to ever get an accurate account of her weight on a standard bathroom scale. "Over four hundred pounds and counting" was the nearest guess that anyone would care to venture—but most cared not to guess at all.

All things considered, however, Didi had a pretty face and, most notably, a cheery disposition. She was also the epitome of a casserole carrying Southern Baptist. A generally devout woman in her late twenties, she was completely sincere in her considerable religious convictions and as a true Christian wished everyone salvation. Most importantly, she was a tolerant woman as well, and for this she was both liked and welcomed everywhere. She was always pleasant.

Didi lived in an old single-wide trailer park about a block from Bo's restaurant with her husband John. People often wondered how they had any room at all in the small eight foot wide trailer because he as notably tall as she was round. John was a fit looking man who worked hard as a truck driver for a local cold rolled steel distributor. He was also a goodly twenty years senior than his wife, and they also had no children.

Didi had met John when she had gone to a local tent revival with a group of other parishioners from her church. He had come in the tent late, drunk beyond caring about anything and, of all things, he plopped

himself down right next to Didi, who was seated at the very end of a row of people she had come with. He said nothing, nor did he pay any attention to the goings on about him in any way. He just slumped back a little, patted his hand on the half-pint of whiskey he had in his right pocket, and finding comfort in that it was still there, quietly dozed off to sleep.

The revival itself had then lasted another two hours with all kinds of singing and testaments to be given, but eventually it was all over, oblivious to John's intermittent snoring. It was when the other folks in her group had gotten up to leave out the far side of the row that Didi had suddenly felt that the Lord had compelled her to say something, right then and there, and so she did.

"Wait a minute. What about this poor fellow here?" Didi called out to the others in her group.

"Oh, just let him sleep it off, can't you see he is nothing but a drunk?" the woman closest to her spoke out.

"I don't know," Didi hesitated. "Don't you think I should wake him up and at least tell him that the revival is over?"

"Didi, would you just let sleeping dogs lie?" another woman who was second in line from the other called back.

"It won't hurt to wake him," Didi responded, ignoring their advice. "Excuse me, sir. The revival is over," she amiably announced, gently tugging a little on the man's shirt sleeve.

"Huh? Oh?" the man said, startled awake by her evocations.

"It's over. Time to go home now," Didi told the man.

"Oh, oh, yeah," the man replied more clearly, making an effort to stand up.

"Are you going to be okay?" Didi asked in concern, standing up to face him straight on.

"Eh, yeah, I just have to get something to eat, that's all," he told her.

"Don't you have anything to eat at home?" Didi asked.

"No, I don't have anything to eat at home," he answered plainly.

"Don't you have a wife to make something?" Didi asked more specifically.

"No," he replied.

"Well, if you want, I could make you something, you know. Besides, it's after ten o'clock now, and there probably isn't anything open."

"That's okay," he answered.

"I live in the Midway Trailer Park just down the street. I don't mind," Didi pressed on.

"Hum, —I am hungry," he said, looking away for a moment in thought.

"Didi, we have to leave now, are you coming or not?" another woman in her group called out in an irritated tone.

"I can take you home. I have my truck outside," the man benignly offered.

"You guys just go on without me, okay?" Didi responded, turning to face every one in the group directly.

"Are you sure?" the same woman condescendingly asked.

"Yes, I'm okay," she affirmed, glancing back at the man who said nothing.

"Okay, we'll look for you in church tomorrow, then," the woman responded in an ominous tone.

And, as all her intentions were good, Didi fed the man who later revealed himself to be called John. To Didi, it was a revelation when not only did John seem to appreciate the meal that she had made for him, and after falling asleep on the couch that evening in her small trailer, he also went to church with her the next morning. Then, for over a month he would religiously stop by after work and she would make him something to eat before leaving to go to his rented room at the local roadside motel.

John was a simple man, and therefore it was hard to tell exactly what his reasoning was for doing anything, for all he did was go to work, come home to drink a half pint of whiskey, and then fall asleep. He was neither good nor bad, sad nor happy, he just was. He offered no opinions about anything and rarely uttered a sentence longer than six words. On Saturday evenings, he budgeted himself enough to go out to the nearest country bar and "tie one on." As a result, this was how he had ended up at the revival.

Didi was totally the opposite. She chatted all the time like a magpie, pleasant enough, but incessantly. Therefore, she was in seventh heaven when John came over because she finally had someone who, she thought, would listen to her ruminations and opinions without interruption. Whether he actually understood what she was talking about, or even tried to, appeared to make no difference to her while he ate his meal in total silence. He never once even asked to have the salt and pepper passed to him. Then, before leaving and after standing up from the small two-seater table, he would customarily tell her, "It was real good," and then finally, "Thank you," just before he left.

Now, if anything, Didi wasn't unimaginative. She was like any other woman who dreamed of being whisked away unto the prince's castle to thereupon surrender herself unto the desires of passion incarnate. Nonetheless, she was a realist as well, figuring that if any time in her life she was going to "get a man," this was it. It was then with a two-fold reasoning that she decided to make her next move. The first reason in her mind was that God had sent him to her so she could save him from his tawdry and sinful life of drinking, and the second one was that, realistically, he might be the only one who "could just might save her" from an ill-fated life of spinsterdom.

So, with all this in mind, and with only a month's acquaintance, Didi decided that since he would probably never ask her, she would have to ask him, "Do you want to get married?"

"Is that what you want?" is all John replied when Didi took it upon herself to "pop the question."

"Yes, that's what I want," Didi answered him as plainly as possible.

"Okay, if that's what you want," John simply accepted. And with no further comment than that, it was a done deal.

It didn't take but two weeks for her to get the license and arrange the small wedding. Neither of them had any relatives present, and besides the preacher himself, the only attendees were a few of her co-workers from the church's day care center where Didi worked. There was no actual honeymoon to speak of, but both were content with their decision, in that neither of them had any intentions of molding the other into something other than what they had always been. John summarily left the motel where he was staying and moved into the little trailer with only a single suitcase of possessions. Didi went on making his meals and doing all the other things involved with keeping the home in good order, while John still went off to work as usual, came back, ate, gave her his paycheck, drank his half pint of whiskey, and then went to bed. She asked to go nowhere, other than to the grocery store, while he continued on with his Saturday evening benders. Nothing at all had substantially changed for either of them, except that they now had each other's company at night to stave off any thoughts of loneliness.

Still in all, Didi began to worry about John's health, for after about six months of seeing him suffer, she now felt that his drinking was killing her man, and in this particular regard she felt that, once again, she had been compelled by the Lord to help him.

"Do you have my money?" John asked on Saturday evening after he had finished his dinner.

"Yes, but I am not going to give it to you," Didi answered unemotionally.

"What?" John asked in surprise.

"You heard me. All you're going to do is drink it up. And even though I don't personally have a problem with that, because after all, I do know it is your money, it is still killing you. Now, as your wife and as God is my witness, I will not give you the money to do it. I refuse to take part in you killing yourself. Therefore no, I am not going to give it to you," Didi categorically declared.

"Who in the hell are you to judge me?" John yelled out at her for the first time since she had known him. "Who in hell are you to judge me?" he repeated again at the top of his lungs as he got up from his chair to physically threatened her face- to-face with his presence.

Now, if it were any other person with any sense at all, you would have thought that the most propitious thing to do was to verily submit to the big lug's demands, but even though Didi had never seen this side of him before, she was not even slightly phased, nor intimidated one iota by his boisterous tirade.

"John, I did not say that you could not have the money," Didi told him evenly, looking directly up at his face looming above her. "I only said that I was not going to give it to you, that's all. If you want the money, you can go to the bookshelf over there and get it yourself," she explicitly pointed out. "In fact, you can take all the money there, if you want. It's in the Bible. Go ahead, take it. But I want you to know—don't look to me for any salvation if you do. And, as far as I'm concerned, if you do, you don't need to come back here, either. Also, I want you to know that I am not going to be yelled at like this again, I can tell you that as well," she stated in an unwavering tone.

"Okay, fine!" John responded flatly, turning to the shelf on the opposite wall from the table.

"There's no going back," Didi warned as John reached up to get the book.

And although those words did not stop John in his tracks, it undoubtedly slowed him down, for then, almost gingerly, he took the

book from its resting place and turned around to once more face Didi again.

"Like I said, you can have the money. Take all of it if you want. Just leave me the Bible, right here on the table, that's all," Didi instructed indifferently, causing him to hesitate for a second and look down at the book in his hand.

"Here, you can have it," John said in a normal volume. "I'm sorry I yelled at you," her husband apologized, putting the Bible directly on the table. "I'm going to bed now," were his final words.

And he did. He also never touched another drink again.

"So you see, that's how the Lord works," Didi spiritedly concluded after reciting "The Testimony of John's Salvation" to Bo, the owner of Charlie's Restaurant.

"That's quite a story," Bo courteously remarked. "Well, it's four o'clock now, and you know the routine. I've got to go back to the kitchen and get set up for dinner. I'll see you tomorrow," he said politely, rising from the booth on his way to do his chores.

"See you tomorrow," Didi responded in kind.

Bo looked forward to Didi coming into his restaurant in the late afternoons, for she was always good-natured, and also loved his food. Her favorite was the foot-long cheese steak sub, and she could verily eat two of them in a row. Although many of the patrons made derogatory comments about her weight, Bo ignored them, for he took her to be more considerate of others than they were considerate of her.

Didi's size was exactly why she came in to eat in the afternoons, for she did not want to cause the gregarious restaurateur any undue hindrance when it was his busy time. She was so large that one of the booth tables had to be completely moved over to the opposite side from where she sat to accommodate her. There was simply no other way to seat her comfortably. Even seating her at one of the center tables wouldn't have

been very prudent either, for a multitude of obvious reasons. Thus, she timed her visits. Her mindfulness in this matter did not go unnoticed by Bo, and so he respectfully went out of his way to accommodate her.

It was perhaps out of fascination more than anything else that Bo began to actually pay attention to her ruminations while taking a break from his afternoon chores. How a person of her girth could get by happily in life simply amazed him. He then made the analogy within his mind that she was the personification of the crippled warrior whose career was considered redundant when he had lost his legs in battle, however, because of his genius as a tactician, he had still become the commander in chief of the kingdom's army. He placed great stock in such a person who could manipulate others by their observational talents and, most importantly, he also knew that such a person could recognize this quality in others.

This is where Bo's conservations with Didi became amusing, because she not only would tell him what was going on in the restaurant "behind his back" when he was not in the dining room, but why the people were doing what they did in the first place. All this was naturally shared with him on a personal basis in the confidence of friendship. It was after six months of this intellectual courtship that Didi also confessed her own true motivations for being there.

"You want to work here? I thought you worked at the church's day care center," Bo asked, not expecting such a question, given Didi's condition and the work involved.

"Actually, I haven't worked there in months. John makes enough for us anyway, so I really don't have to work at all, —but I want to work here. You see, I've always wanted to cook in a restaurant. It's one of my dreams," Didi revealed like a girl asking her father for a pony. "You won't have to pay me much. I'll work for minimum wage," she offered as seductively as she could.

"Oh, my God," was the only phrase that came to Bo's mind as he fought to think of an acceptable response, one that would not offend her. On one hand, he genuinely liked her, but on the other, he knew that it was he who was the target now of her manipulative proclivities, and that wasn't so palatable at all. Still, there were other factors that had to be weighed. He admired the orchestration of her campaign, right down to the finesse of her delivery. This took planning, patience, and above all, never losing sight of her goal. All this, now went through Bo's brain in an instant as he still searched for a gracious way out.

"Well, what do you think you can do?" Bo reacted more than questioned, hoping to have a few more moments to think.

"Cook, of course," Didi said succinctly. "Or, I can put the stuff together ahead of time, so you can just heat it up," she further offered brightly. "I can make chicken and dumplings. I can make some macaroni casserole. I can even make the meatloaf, if you give me your recipe. I can even just clean up back there for you, you know, like put away everything you get out for lunchtime and then get everything ready for dinner. I don't need a lot of hours, just a few in the afternoon, that's all. Then you will have some more time to get your paperwork done, or even go to the bank if you need to," she suggested, again in her trademarked cheerful manner.

"Well, I guess I might be able give you a few hours," Bo considerately replied, "But the problem is I don't think that you can physically do it," he recanted, more as a challenge than a denial, believing he had shrewdly found a way out of granting her request by being as straightforward and honest as possible.

"Oh, just because I'm fat doesn't mean that I can't move," Didi declared with no modesty whatsoever.

"Oh no, that's not what I mean at all, Didi," Bo respectfully responded in clarification. "Come here, I'll show you what I mean," he offered

with his right hand out to lead the way. "See, this is what I mean," he specifically pointed out as soon as they had gotten into the kitchen.

What Bo showed Didi then was simply a fact, as he saw it. The cooking equipment, such as the stove, grill, and fry-o-lators were all lined up in the small kitchen against the back wall, and directly in front of them was the pick-up counter. To the left side wall and directly opposite the side of the pick-up counter stood a tall white reach-in refrigerator whose door faced the cooking line for easy access. This alone had become Didi's "straits of adversity" now, for the opening between the pick-up counter and the side of the refrigerator was at most, a foot wide. Even Bo had to turn sideways to pass through it. Thus, as Bo had it figured, there would be no possible way that Didi could pass through it herself, and consequently he was saved from becoming "The Dream Killer."

"So, here is the problem, Didi," Bo factually presented. "I guess I could give you some hours, but the only problem is, —is that I don't that think you can get back there to do the job," he proposed in a regretful tone.

"Can I at least try?" Didi asked politely, clearly not willing to give up her heart's desire so easily, when finally it seemed within her grasp.

"Sure, you can try," Bo told her agreeably, "but don't knock the dishes off the top of the shelf," he warned.

"Okay," she answered, going over to the small opening with all the brightness endemic to her persona.

Even turning sideways however, her efforts were fruitless. And when the shelving on top of the counter started to shake, and the dishes began to rattle, she had to back off, being both exasperated and sadly dejected in her failed attempt to breach the obstacle that kept her heart's desire out of reach.

"Oh well, —I understand," Didi said in disappointment, while Bo watched her usually exuberant spirit evaporate before his eyes.

"You know, Didi, if you just lost a few pounds you could probably fit back there," Bo mentioned empathetically in trying to soothe her anguish. "I'll tell you what, I'll make you a deal, —the day you can fit back there, you got job. Now, mind you, it would only be in the afternoons for about three hours at minimum wage, but just the same, that's the deal. Okay?" he considerately proposed, even though he still believed that his offer would never come to fruition.

"Okay," accepted Didi, perking up and flashing Bo a small and determined smile.

Bo, having thought the whole situation had been completely put to rest, and after dismissing it entirely from his mind, suddenly found out quite differently about three weeks later.

"Bo, Didi is in the kitchen, I just thought you'd might like to know," Betty announced forebodingly the instant Bo had come back through the front door from his afternoon trip to the bank.

"How long has she been there?" Bo asked, clearly startled by the unexpected news.

"Oh, about fifteen minutes or so," Betty responded with the slyest of grins, continuing to clear off one of the booths.

"Well, could you put the deposit bag away for me?" Bo asked, placing it on the end of the eat-on counter on his way to the kitchen.

"Sure, no problem," Betty grinned again.

"Hello, Bo, what do you think?" Didi elatedly greeted, standing from behind the pick-up counter with a large wooden spoon raised high in the air, as if it was a torch of victory.

"Well, I see you made it," Bo commented in light surprise. "So, if you don't mind, how did you ever get back there? That's all I want to know," he both asked and stated at the same time

"Here, I'll show you," Didi said, putting down her scepter with the smugness of success.

It was then that Bo saw something that he never could have imagined, nor ever wanted to see again. Very methodically Didi reached down and started to roll up the hem of her Mumu styled dress until it reached under her pendulous breasts and tucked it there. She then reached down again and, hand-over-hand, gathered up the huge sections of human flab that hung copiously off her frame like an overflowing cauldron of excessively risen dough. Fold by fold, she collected this great mass until, in one great "harrumph," she flopped it down right on top of the end of the counter. Then, tippy-toeing, in almost a jaunting fashion, she squeezed past the refrigerator with her back to it while literally dragging the mound of flesh across the counter top with her as she went. Finally, in one giant "oofff," she made it past the end of the counter as the whole assemblage of blubber fell back again against her knees. Then, as her Mumu came tumbling down after raising her arms straight into the air, she triumphantly questioned, "So, what do you think, Bo?" beaming from ear to ear.

"I don't know what to think, Didi," Bo responded, befuddled as never before.

"I do have a job now, don't I?" Didi said with an expectant smile.

"Eh, —yeah, sure, —yeah," Bo all but mumbled, still in a daze from having witnessed the most graphic demonstration, that in his wildest dreams, could ever have been imagined.

"Oh, what the hell," was what Bo almost really said, but he did not, —not only out of respect for her religious convictions, but that such a comment would also be demeaning to his dignity as well. He prided himself in being a man of his word, and besides, "maybe this will be a good thing," he concluded in keeping his word.

And pretty much, it was. Didi had become an invaluable deterrent for him against the grueling monotony of having to put in a twelve hour

work day, week after week, even without a mid-day break. Bo had now even joined a local health spa with another couple of restaurant owners who had the same schedule as he, and for the first time since he had opened the place, felt comfortable that it wouldn't descend into chaos if he wasn't constantly there.

For over three months, this arrangement went on as agreed until one Wednesday afternoon, after returning from his trip to the spa, Betty said "You better see the kitchen" in a most foreboding tone.

"What the hell happened here?" Bo exclaimed after entering the kitchen with Betty close behind. "And where is Didi?" he asked further, noticing that all of the dishes had been knocked off the pick-up counter shelving, landing the floor to shatter in pieces. He even noticed that the entire counter had been pushed askew from its former position, as well.

"You know the last time that the pest control man was here?" Betty asked as a reminder.

"Yeah, I remember," Bo said in an unhappy tone.

"And he put out some of that poison around to take care of any mice or rats that might get in?" Betty further questioned.

"Yeah, go on," Bo prompted impatiently.

"Well, I guess we did have a rat, and it came out and scared her," Betty told him plainly, for although she did feel quite bad for Didi, she personally had no such fears.

"Oh, my God," Bo said out loud, paused to think for a second. "Now besides cleaning up this place, what do you think I should do?" he solicited, while still surveying the damage.

"Well, if it were me, I don't think I would do anything right now, at least as far as Didi is concerned. You might just make the whole thing worse," Betty advised.

"Yeah, I guess you are right," Bo agreed. "I think I'll just wait until Didi comes back by herself, that's all," he openly concluded. "Meanwhile, I'm going to have to clean this mess up, and I guess if

she doesn't come back by the weekend, then I'll go over to her trailer and see how she is. She doesn't have a phone," he continued to ramble, as the room's devastation was still usurping his attention. "So, she was pretty frightened, huh?" he then asked in genuine concern.

"I'd say so," Betty unequivocally confirmed.

And as suspected, the weekend had come and gone without having heard a single word from Didi, and so when Bo had left work on that next Monday morning, he was coming with the notion of paying her a visit sometime in the afternoon. This made no difference however, for Didi was unexpectedly already waiting for him, right by the front door, as soon as he arrived to open.

"So how are you feeling, Didi? Are you okay?" Bo asked compassionately, as soon as he approached her.

"Yeah, I'm fine now, but I have to talk with you," Didi somberly replied.

"Sure, just let me open up the door first," Bo said. "Come on, let's go over here and sit down," he offered, going over to one of the free standing tables where they could be seated comfortably.

"So, you're okay then?" Bo asked Didi again politely, once seated.

"Yeah, I'm okay. But I can't work here anymore," Didi somberly stated with a profound sadness.

"I understand," replied Bo, respectfully.

"No, I don't think you do," Didi said leadingly.

"Well, tell me," Bo politely asked. "You can tell me," he then cajoled in a friendly and confidential manner, for Didi appeared to have some hesitation.

"Okay, I'll tell you," Didi began. "You see, it's like this: it wasn't seeing the rat that bothered me. Aw, come on, Bo, let's face it, I live in an old dumpy trailer park. I've seen rats before," she admitted off-

handedly, beginning to relax a little. But that's not it at all," she paused for a second to see if she had his full attention.

"It wasn't?" responded Bo.

"No, it wasn't," Didi said flatly in response. "Let me tell you what actually happened," she began to confess. "First of all, I had made a cheesesteak sandwich for someone who was sitting at the counter, so I put it in the pass-through window instead of on the pickup counter. And then, just after doing that, I looked up and saw one of the fattest and biggest rats that I've ever seen, crawling on the electrical pipe that runs along the ceiling over the window.

"Then, when I looked at him closer, he wasn't moving so fast, like they usually do. This one looked like he was drunk, while he sort of just waddled along the top of the pipe. I guess he must have been poisoned and was dying, I figured. But that didn't make any difference!" Didi then blurted out in sudden burst of defiance. "He was still after the cheesesteak I had put in the window! So, slowly, I reached back over to get it, and then all of a sudden, as soon I got my hand on the plate, he fell off the pipe and landed smack, right on my arm!" she all but exclaimed as her eyes widened in the reliving of the horrifying experience. "And then it just laid there," she said in complete and utter distress. "It didn't even fall off or anything. It just laid there, —looking right at me with those beady little eyes and his little tongue sticking out too. Oh, my God, it was terrible!" she exclaimed, pausing for a second in taking a deep breath, while Bo only sat there in dead silence, trying to take it all in.

"But that still wasn't the worst of it, either," Didi began again, shaking her head. "Then, it was if the rat had started to talk to me. I could hear him. I could hear him talking right to me," she testified as if she was speaking at a revival. "He told me that he really didn't care if he died. He told me that he knew that he was poisoned, but still, the only thing that he wanted before he died was my sandwich. Oh, my God Bo, don't you see, I could hear him because I have become nothing more

than a fat rat too!" she had concluded in a sad and tortured acceptance of her fate. "So, you do understand why I can't work here anymore, don't you?" she then tenderly asked in a desperate bid to receive some kind of solace from the one person in the world, besides he husband, that cared for her welfare.

"I understand, Didi," Bo responded graciously. "But you will stop by for a visit once in a while, won't you?" he added in an affectionate tone.

"Of course I will," she finally smiled, recognizing their mutual respect.

But Bo was never to see Didi again, as she and her husband had summarily vanished from the Midway Trailer Park that day. He did, however, get word of what happened to her from one of the other folks who still lived in the park. Apparently, John, her reformed husband, had told her that they had to move. He told her that the same Lord that had saved him from his suffering, was still the same Lord that told him that he had to take her to a place which was too far for her to walk to the nearest restaurant, or grocery store, —and if he did not, he quoted to her utter amazement, then "The drunkard and the glutton shall come unto poverty."

Scientifically Wise

Willa Cleary was the slightest of things, with long honey colored hair and freckles. Her father was bookkeeper who earned a steady living at a local meat packing plant in the middle of rural nowhere, and her mother was the local high school music teacher. For reasons unknown, Willa was an only child, and the three of them lived peacefully on the outskirts of town in a small wood-frame house. It was a quaint little house that sat by itself on a ten acre parcel that her father had inherited from his grandmother.

Willa had always been taken both to and from school by her mother, and because of her naturally quiet disposition, she never really developed any personal relationships with any of the other students, either in or out of the teaching institution. She was a book worm, and she was a happy bookworm at that. She went to school as required, but that was about it. She read books because she liked to, not because she was told to.

Everything important in life could be found in a book, Willa thought. And what couldn't, could be imagined. Therefore, all three of them, — she, her books, and her imagination, all became one happy family unto itself. She had read Anne of Green Gables several times and toyed with reading one of the Hardy Boys series for balance, but never quite got around to it. Instead, she opted for Agatha Christie.

Willa had also found non-fiction interesting as well. When she came to a word that described a certain fabric, she had to read all about how it was made. When she came to another word that described a style of architecture, she had to look it up, too. Then, one afternoon when a book used the genus name for a certain flower, she not only looked it up in an encyclopedia to get its complete definition, but had gotten a revelation when she did. "If all of the information necessary to grow these flowers can simply be found in a book, why can't I grow them myself? After all, I have a whole ten acres to work with," she thought. So, beginning with

only the general implements of yard tending tools, Willa went about her task of converting the entirety of the property into her own personal flower garden, complete with a whole colony of fairies that kept her company while she worked.

Eventually, after a multitude of uneventful seasons had passed, Willa turned eighteen and had graduated high school. Besides becoming taller, perhaps a little taller than most girls, she looked no different than when she was a little girl. Spindly, and still with her long blond hair streaming down her back, she considered herself a "naturalist." She even had secretly named herself the Willowing Willa as she confabulated with her plants and fairies on a regular basis. She was quite content with herself as she was, wished to go nowhere, and accepted where she lived as her destiny. It might have taken her years of growing up to convert the entire ten acres into the most phenomenal "back yard garden" ever to step foot on, but with only an occasional helping hand from her father, she did all the work herself.

After graduation, with a courteous nod to her mother, Willa was able to obtain employment in the local county library as a library assistant. Her primary job was to put away the returned books, catalogue the new ones that came in, and then work in the "books by mail" department. She said little to anyone, and as her job did not require it, her job was a perfect fit.

She had bought herself a small Datsun pickup truck to not only go back and forth to work with, but to use for her gardening purposes as well. She also had joined the county's official gardening club. This, in essence, was her only social link to the outside social world, although she never thought of looking at it in that manner. To her, she only joined so that she might learn some first-hand gardening techniques which she knew could never be learned from a book.

It was there that she met Sean O'Connor, another of her Irish kinsmen. Sean had taken the scientific approach to gardening. "Chemicals, and all

that stuff," Willa would articulate disapprovingly whenever she got into a conversation about Sean's chosen methods. Nonetheless, they were colleagues, and although they had completely opposite points of view, they both were well respected in the world of home grown horticulture for their notable successes. What she did not produce in bounty as he did, she produced in beauty and variety.

Sean was almost as much of a loner as Willa. Where Willa's only interface with the scholastic world in high school was her favorite English teacher, Sean's was his chemistry teacher. He wasn't necessarily a quiet person, but he generally only spoke to those who were in his field of interest. A tallish, curly headed boy who wore a pair of horned rimmed glasses, invariably a brown checkered shirt of some variety, and looked exactly what a chemistry student was imagined to look like, if not a budding engineer. He, unlike Willa, was not an only child. He had two other brothers and a sister, however, they were nothing like him in temperament, and for most of his leisure time he stayed to himself. In this he was no different than Willa at all.

His family owned a small sixty acre farm which was completely dedicated to the growing of both blueberries and strawberries. Here, Sean was allowed to build himself a large greenhouse on the property where he experimented with hydroponics and the growing of exotic flowers, such as orchids, for the local flower shops and funeral homes. This is where he received his own personal spending money. He had graduated from the same high school two years earlier than Willa, but neither of them had met before they both had become members of the garden club.

"I noticed your sunflowers when I drove past your place last weekend. They are the tallest and largest I've ever seen," Sean told Willa one day after a garden club meeting.

"Yes, they are beautiful, aren't they?" Willa said with proud smile.

"So, what did you think about the orchids that I brought to the club the last time?" Sean questioned.

"Oh, I thought they were quite also beautiful," Willa politely responded in kind, but with less enthusiasm.

"Well you say that, but somehow I get from the tone in your voice that you also have another opinion, too. You can tell me, I won't be offended," Sean told her with a shrug.

"Okay, if you want," Willa replied in a forewarning tone.

"Okay, then, —go ahead," he prompted, spreading out his hands as if to say, "So give me a shot, I can take it."

"It's just that, you see, I know you use all those chemicals, and I believe that it takes away something from the natural growth of the plants," Willa broke loose from her usually guarded opinions in a tumble of impassioned words. "Sure, your orchids are beautiful enough, but to me, they don't have the same smell, —to me, they practically don't have any smell at all! They are like those roses in the flower shops that are rehydrated after they get them from South America. Then, before they deliver them, they have to spray them with that fake rose smell they buy. How terrible is that," she said in no uncertain terms, shaking her head in disgust and disapproval.

"So you know about that?" Sean replied in a state of mild surprise.

"Oh yeah, of course I know about it," Willa stated more than admitted.

"Well, then you must know it, too, —that they can't do it any other way, especially if they are going to make any kind profit, don't you?" Sean questioned further.

"Yeah, I realize that, and that's why I usually don't offer my opinion to anyone in the first place. I know to most of the folks that it's all about the money, but not me. I love my plants for who they are, and not what they are," Willa enlightened him.

And as all things have a beginning born out of conflict, so it was for the birth of their relationship, each sharing the quest to submit the other unto their own way of thinking. Polite as ever, but as unyielding as an oak tree in a rain storm, each of them now began their own campaign to convert the other. The only problem that they encountered was that there was simply not enough time at the garden club meetings for either of them to sufficiently gain any ground. It was then, after this annoying issue seemed to have no imminent solution that Sean suggested that the two of them meet at Charlie's Restaurant after the Garden Club meetings were over. There they could hash things out.

"So you say that your plants are a who, and not a what?" Sean revisited after they both had ordered what they wanted at their first unrestricted encounter.

"They all have names, don't they?" Willa put to him.

"As a classification, they do," Sean ceded specifically.

"Mine also have first names, too. Don't any of yours?" Willa asked directly, arching one of her eyebrows for effect.

"No, of course not, they're plants," Sean flatly replied. "They already have a botanical name. What else is necessary?" he added dispassionately, looking straight back at her and cocking his head.

"You mean to tell me that you don't have a special name for at least one of your plants?" Willa grilled him to the point of testing his truthfulness.

"Well, I guess I can tell you. I do refer to my Venus Fly Trap 'Psyche.' But that's only for fun," Sean confessed.

"Oh, how interesting is that?" Willa smiled wryly while her adversary had nothing more to say.

And so it went for about and hour, until Sean had finished his cheeseburger and Willa her salad.

It was on the way home that Willa thought of the meeting as her very first social encounter. She was tickled by Sean's timidity when

challenged. She was also impressed by his honesty. "Maybe having someone to talk to might not be so bad?" she considered, as she already invited him to come over to see her garden first hand. No one, in any manner, had ever been invited to see her garden before. Aside from her mother coming to visit her once in a while, the garden was her sole domain, and her domain alone. It was there that she had spent most of her personal time by herself, either reading or gardening, —or so everyone thought.

"This is quite some place," Sean told her in stepping into her Elizabethan gazebo in the middle of her garden on that following Saturday morning.

"Thank you. I call it 'Fairy Haven,' for it is home to one of the largest fairy colonies in the whole county," Willa said with a smile, putting down the book she was reading on the small wicker end table to her right.

"You're kidding me, right?" Sean questioned with a facetious grin.

"No, not at all," Willa answered brightly, rising from her matching wicker chair. "You see that dwarf cherry tree over there?"

"Yeah, I see it," Sean acknowledged.

"That's their favorite place of all, Willa commented. "In the evening, when the sun is beginning to set, they gather there to watch it go down. That is when I read them some passages from Keats. They like that. Of course, sometimes they actually like to hear Milton too, for some strange reason that I really can't figure out, but I read it to them just the same."

"So, —you really think that these fairies are actually out there?" Sean questioned in total disbelief.

"Of course they are. Don't you believe in fairies? You're an O'Connor, aren't you?" Willa rhetorically questioned, referring to his Irish heritage. "You mean to tell me that you don't believe in leprechauns, or kissing the Blarney Stone for good luck, either?" Willa additionally pressed on.

"Listen, I grant you that believing in all that stuff might make you feel better, but even you must know that there is no scientific evidence that things such as fairies, elves, or even gnomes exist, —don't you?" Sean pointedly questioned, while pertinaciously crossing his arms.

"No, I do not," Willa told him distinctly, her ire rising like a tempest out of nowhere. "And you can't prove to me scientifically that they don't, either," she snipped back while wagging her finger directly in front of his face.

"Well, you got me there," Sean conceded with an acquiescent smile, unfolding his arms with his palms up in surrender.

"So, now that we got that over with, do you want to see the rest of the place?" Willa cordially offered with a soft smile, content for the time being with Sean's capitulation.

"Okay, just show me the way," Sean assented with small shrug and a thin smile of his own.

"This ought to be interesting," Sean thought, taking notice that beneath the wide-brimmed straw hat Willa was wearing and below the flowered summer dress she had on, was a pair of high topped and tightly laced work boots.

"First of all, I want to take you to see my livestock," Willa told him as she led the way.

"You mean you have livestock, too?" Sean asked in surprise.

"You have to, if you are going to have a successful natural garden," Willa told him mindfully while passing right under the Cherry Tree of Fairies. "Well, here it is," she declared. "The home of Benjamin Bunny and his family of furry friends."

"What is this, a rabbit hutch?" Sean asked.

"Oh, it's more than that," Willa said. "It's a home. You see, he has his own fenced in yard. He has his own village water tower that keeps the water trough full, and his own private quarters too. You see the biggest cubby over there, up on top of that big stilt platform?" she pointed out,

"that's for him and his mate," she clarified. "And over there on the other side of the platform are all the other cubbies for the rest of his family. Now, you see that ramp over there?" she then nodded directionally.

"Yeah, I see it," Sean acknowledged.

"That is how they get up there," Willa annotated. "Now, of course this is a working village," she stated. "In return for all of the clippings I get from my garden, and sometimes a treat, of course, they give me their pellets in return. Those I use for my fertilizer. See, the front floor of the platform is made out of hardware cloth, which lets the pellets fall down onto a tray underneath. It's all very simple, don't you think?" she asked in a rare moment of pride.

"I guess that's one way of doing it," Sean amicably ratified.

"I've been working on this garden since I was a little girl," Willa mentioned, now walking along the path between the vegetable and flower planters alike. "Everything here I made myself, except for the gazebo. That, my dad built for me. He even ran some electric out here so I would have a light to read by if I came out here at night. Sometimes, I just sit here and look up at the stars. Those you can see better without the light," she noted.

"Yeah, I know," Sean agreed.

"But, like I said before, the best time to come out here though is when the sun is going down, for that's the best time to see the fairies," Willa doggedly reasserted, only this time with a broad grin.

It was quite an interesting combination, the rest of the garden club thought, watching the two opposites becoming fast friends. They constantly argued about all kinds of things, like a couple of antagonist lawyers who had gone to the same college, but then, after a day of challenging each other in court, ended up drinking at the same bar together. Most of all, their arguments were centered about philosophical differences, for he was still of the mindset that all things could be

accounted for through science, and she was of the mindset that there were still plenty of things that science would never be able to prove.

Still in all, it wasn't Sean's success as a scientific farmer that she was constantly at odds with, and it wasn't the use of his "unnatural chemicals" that really drove her crazy. It was the fact that he would not yield one inch that a garden had no other purpose to exist than to raise things for a profit. Nonetheless, she had the fairies on her side, and sooner or later, she figured, he would have to succumb to their powers.

"What is the difference if I buy my fertilizer at the fertilizer plant or you use your rabbit pellets? It is all the same nitrogen!" Sean argued one day.

"No, it isn't," Willa defiantly stood her ground. "My fertilizer is natural, yours has no life to it. Yours is dead. Just like the flavor is in those tomatoes you grow. You know, those tomatoes that you keep on life support, the ones that you raise in a coma," Willa argued back with a vengeance.

"I don't see anyone complaining at the grocery store," Sean noted cavalierly. "And by the way, that's why I have a new full sized pickup, and you are still driving that old toy Datsun of yours," he self-justified.

"I don't need, nor do I want, to drive that thing you drive. I like my little truck. We are friends. I put my own sachet in it, so it smells nice, — not like that old vinyl and Armor-All smell that your truck smells like," Willa fired back. "Besides, the fairies don't like that smell, either. They say it's unnatural," she deliberately taunted again with a grin, full well knowing such comments would bumfuzzle him to no end.

Such were the conversations under the gazebo, week after week, as Willa grew even more determined to make Sean see the world through her eyes. She even began to call him diggers, as he said his parents did, in a deliberate attempt to make him more receptive to the efficacy of her suggestions. There was no doubt about it, she felt that she, as well as

everyone else, was part and parcel of a greater collective of spirits, and whether anyone besides herself admitted it or not, she wholeheartedly believed this. Likewise, she reckoned that only some folks could actually see these spirits, and in her specific case, the fairies in her garden, —but others could not. This, she also verily accepted to be true, but did not know why. Nor did she dwell on it, either.

Nonetheless, Willa tirelessly tried everything she could to help Sean become one with the fairies. When he came over, she made him tea from the chamomile plants that she grew in her own garden. She hung small sachet bags made from the flowers in her garden off the rafters of the gazebo so that he could breathe in the scents that she thought attracted the fairies to her garden in the first place. She even asked him to pet her bunny rabbits when he came over, so they would get used to his presence and not cause them to have any anxieties when he came over. Her real purpose, however, was that she also believed that her rabbits were magical too, and thus the watchful fairies would take kindly to this gesture.

Although Sean thought that Willa was "kind of nutty," she thoroughly fascinated him. Being a "scientific person," he simply came to the conclusion that the feminine persuasion could not be explained under any known structured methodology, any more than things like love, passion, and yes, her fairies. Just the same, he could not explain his fondness for her, either. All he knew was that she made him feel good when he was with her. She made him feel like a human being first, and a research person second, not the other way around. And if there was only one thing that pleased him the most about her, that was it.

After about six months, and despite their opposite points of view, they were now seeing each other on a regular basis. For the most part, however, it was he who came to visit her in the evenings underneath the sanctity of her garden's gazebo. She in turn provided him with his very own wicker chair to sit upon.

"There is going to be a meteor shower this Friday night," Sean informed her one April evening after he had just come over to her place.

"Oh, yeah?" Willa asked in interest, her eyes lighting up at the prospect.

"Yeah, about nine o'clock or so. It should last about at least a half an hour, they say," Sean added, smiling at her reaction.

"I'd like to see that. Do you want to come over here so we can watch it from my garden?" Willa asked.

"Sure, about seven-thirty, eight?" Sean proposed.

"Yeah, that's fine. I'll get my hibachi out and we can grill some hot dogs. How about that?" Willa offered.

"Sure, that'll be good. I'll stop and get some Fritos or something and bring over my cooler with some soda too," Sean suggested.

"Oh, the Fritos are okay, but I'll make some ice tea. I'd rather have that," Willa submitted.

"Okay, that's fine by me," Sean agreeably accepted.

And as the appointed time came on that clear and starry night had come around, Willa had put out a couple of folding chairs out on the mulched walkway area next to where the cherry tree stood so that they could get a better view of the heavens above. She also had put a short stack of cinder blocks in front of the chairs to be used as a temporary table for her hibachi and sundry picnicking utensils, along with bottle of ketchup for her, and a bottle of mustard for him. She even brought out one of her parent's folding TV tables, setting it between the two chairs, while on top of it she placed a pitcher of ice tea that was accompanied by two plastic tumblers filled with ice.

"So this is it?" Shaun asked, approaching the small campestral viewing area.

"Yup, here we are," Willa cheerfully replied, all dressed up as if she was a girl in a Renaissance Fair, complete with a crown of flowers set in her hair.

"What? Is this going to be like a Stonehenge festival or something?" Sean teased.

"Exactly," Willa replied, ignoring his obvious provocation while she flitted over to where he was standing, captured up the bag of Fritos he had dangling from his hand, turned, and put it down next to the pitcher of tea.

"This is supposed to be a scientific observation," Sean offered in clarification, according to his point of view.

"Oh, pish-tosh," Willa dramatically waved her hands and grinned, unaffected by Sean's stodginess. "Come on, sit down, get comfortable," she told him with a light smile. "The sun will be going down, and that's the best time to see the fairies. That is, of course, if you are a believer," she needled him with a provocative grin.

"Oh, well I guess we'll see, won't we?" Sean delicately acquiesced, efficiently taking his seat in a feeble attempt to resist her effervescent sprightliness.

"The hot dogs are in that plastic container next to the hibachi by the utensils," Willa casually mentioned, also taking her seat. "Do you want to put them on, or do you want me to?" she courteously asked.

"I can do that. You open the Fritos and pour the tea, then, okay?" Sean replied, reaching down to get the hot dogs.

It was a quiet evening as the two of them passed the time by exchanging their past experiences of attending the county fairs and the Fourth of July celebrations. Neither of them had ever talked to anyone about these personal experiences, for neither of them ever had a close friend to share them with. But now everything was different as they waited in together for the sunset to wain into the darkness of the night in the hopeful expectation of witnessing the glory of a shooting star.

"Well, there are the fairies!" Willa all of a sudden announced, pointing to the cherry tree beside them. "You see them dancing on the branches there? Like I told you before, this is the best time to see them,

at sunset," Willa happily exclaimed. "Don't you see them on the top of the branches?" she blithely asked again.

"I don't see anything," Sean replied, now actually looking over to the tree.

"There they are, over there on the top side, facing the sun," Willa pointed out.

"Oh, that's just the breeze moving the leaves and reflecting the light, that's all that is," Sean rejected.

"No, it isn't," Willa disagreed resolutely. "It's the fairies dancing about to the setting of the sun."

"Well, let's just see," said Sean, rising from his chair and directly going over to the tree. "Okay fairies, come out, come out wherever you are!" he called as he grasped onto one of the lower hanging branches and shook it. "Oh God, I guess I shouldn't have done that!" he suddenly cried out as a rainfall of dried up cherry blossom husks fell upon him. "All that stuff is in my hair now," Sean complained in destress, stumbling erratically as he came out from under the tree while trying to brush himself off in a fervor.

"You shouldn't have done that," Willa laughed in vindication.

"Yeah, I know. It's all over me. I'm going to need a real shower now, not just a meteor shower," Sean replied in good sport.

"You're going to need more than that," Willa grinned.

"What do you mean?" Sean questioned.

"Just so that you know, there was more than just the cherry blossom husks that fell all over you," Willa informed him. "There was a whole lot of was fairy dust, too. They don't like to be shaken off their tree like that. I'm afraid they've put a spell of bad luck upon you now, —and that you can't wash off," she warned forebodingly. "Somehow, you are going to have make amends or feel the consequences," Willa further cautioned, looking up at him with her eyebrows raised.

"Oh, it's like you said before, 'Pish-tosh' —let the fairies get used to it. That's what I say," Sean mimicked in total unconcern, retaking his seat.

"Well, I wouldn't have said that, either. You know they can hear you, don't you?" Willa warned again.

"Like I said, —oh, pish-tosh," Sean dismissively repeated with a wave of his hand.

Regardless, their astrological undertaking turned out to be quite the sight to see that night as the meteors showered down upon them in a continuous stream of brightly colored streaks across the pitch black sky. Then, eventually, after a total of four hot dogs were consumed, along with the entire bag of Fritos and a full gallon of ice tea, the sighting came to an end. All in all, they both agreed that this would be an unforgettable event, whereupon Sean got back in his truck and went home. Willa went back over to the hibachi, doused it with a watering can, looked over to the cherry tree, said "sorry," and then summarily went to bed.

"I thought you had to run some errands for your father this morning," Willa said in surprise, seeing Sean come into her garden the very next day, after having left it not six hours earlier.

"Here, I brought you something," was Sean's first statement, approaching her with a large brown burlap bag clasped firmly in his right hand.

"It is that so important that you had to come here this early?" Willa questioned in a mystified tone.

"I still have some errands to run, but yes, this is more important," Sean stipulated. "Go on, take a look," he said, handing out the weighty bag.

"Oh, what's this? You brought me a big rock, is that it?" Willa remarked satirically, after putting the bag on the ground and looking inside.

"No, go ahead and take it out," Sean explicitly pressed her.

"Okay," Willa replied with a shrug, bending down and with both hands to lift out the cantaloupe sized object from the bag.

"So, what do you think?" Sean asked, after Willa had studied the hefty stone-like article.

"Like I said, what is it, some kind of big rock? I don't know. Why don't you tell me?" Willa cluelessly proposed.

"It's a meteor, silly," Sean said with a smile. "It's probably made of iron. That's why it's so heavy. See all those craters on it? That's because it was so hot when it came down that its impurities were bubbling up to its surface," he explained scientifically.

"Oh yeah, I see them. And look at this," Willa showed him, turning the meteor around so he could observe what she had noticed. "See those two larger crater holes?" she asked.

"Yeah, I see them," Sean said.

"So, now if you look at this kind of crevasse underneath it, it looks like it's smiling at you, see?" Willa lightly smiled herself, adjusting the meteor so he could better see what she was pointing out.

"More like laughing, I would say," Sean responded wistfully, taking back his prize to study it more intently.

"What do mean by that?" Willa questioned perplexedly.

"Well, —I guess the first thing I have to tell you is that I am never going to shake that fairy tree of yours ever again,—no siree, Bob. That I can absolutely tell you," Sean distinctly stressed. "And the second thing is," he continued, "is that it just didn't land on my farm. It landed right on top of my greenhouse," he finally disclosed, pausing for a moment to see her reaction.

"Oh, wow," Willa responded, completely taken aback as her eyes widened in astonishment.

"Yeah, and it took out the whole main section of my hydroponic growing system, besides making about a three foot hole in ground too," Sean testified.

"That's terrible," Willa said compassionately.

"Yeah, I know," he mourned in agreement. "But anyway, it still isn't something that I can't repair," Sean noted on the bright side.

"Don't worry, I bet you'll have it fixed in no time," Willa told him cheerfully. "Then you'll feel better," she predicted.

"Maybe with your help I will," Sean then strangely proffered.

"What do you mean? I don't know how to repair a greenhouse," Willa haplessly asserted.

"It's not the greenhouse that I need your help with," Sean informed her.

"It's not?" Willa responded.

"No, it's not," Sean replied succinctly. Then, after a heavy sigh, and pausing for a short second, he said, "I need to you intercede for me with the fairies. That's what I need. Would you?" he now asked in a most humble manner.

"Are you kidding me?" Willa asked in utter disbelief, while failing to hide the subtle grin within her.

"Well, maybe you can start by letting me put this meteor under their cherry tree over there," Sean suggested, glanced down for a second at the fallen star still tightly clasped within his hands.

"But it's your meteor," Willa asserted, divinely believing that it was meant to be his.

"Nope, I'm giving it to the fairies," Sean firmly ruled, looking back at Willa. "Maybe —just maybe, they'll forgive me for shaking their tree," he proposed.

"Forgiveness is unnecessary once faith is achieved," replied Willa.

Other Publications by J.L. Baumann

Annie Russo - Tenacity Born

Mountain Spirits Speak

A Variety of Passion

A Gothic Rendezvous

Sonnets of the Provocative Kind

Farm Fantasies and Figments of Imagination

Mackenzie Goes Adventuring

Chickens Say What?

Chickens Say Que?